Symbols That Stand for Themselves

Symbols That Stand for Themselves

ROY WAGNER

THE UNIVERSITY OF CHICAGO PRESS
Chicago and London

Roy Wagner is professor of anthropology at the University of Virginia. He is the author of *The Invention of Culture, Habu: The Innovation of Meaning in Daribi Religion,* and *The Curse of Souw,* all published by the University of Chicago Press, and of *Lethal Speech.*

The University of Chicago Press, Chicago 60637
The University of Chicago Press, Ltd., London
© 1986 by The University of Chicago
All rights reserved. Published 1986
Printed in the United States of America

95   94   93   92   91   90   89   88   87   5432

Library of Congress Cataloging-in-Publication Data

Wagner, Roy.
        Symbols that stand for themselves.

        Sequel to: The invention of culture.
        Bibliography: p.
        Includes index.
        1 Symbolism.   2 Culture.   3 Meaning (Psychology)
4 Daribi.   I. Wagner, Roy.   Invention of culture.
II. Title.
GN452.5.W33   1986   306   85-16448
ISBN 0-226-86928-8
ISBN 0-226-86929-6 (pbk.)

To my son, Jonathan

Contents

Preface

This is a book about meaning as the constitutive and organizing power in cultural life. Its argument is that the human phenomenon is a single, coherent idea, organized mentally, physically, and culturally around the form of perception that we call "meaning." This idea allows a simple and unified unfolding perspective in place of the explanatory mosaic generated by the accidental collision of a known general phenomenon with particular academic subject areas. Trope, or metaphor—just precisely that aspect of expression that is least tangible or glossable—amounts to the germ of a pervasive processual tendency. A kind of involution of self-reference, the tendency is formal and systematic over and above particular symbolic contents.

Meaning is not, of course, a free-floating intangible, but a phenomenon that stands in a certain relation to the conventions of culture. Just how it does so, in what ways, and through what forms of mediation, has long been a subject of speculation and controversy. Most attempts at resolution have been anxious to anchor the phenomenon amid the manipulable and the accessible—the syntaxes, grammars, and categories of saying, the necessity and productivity of doing.

Clearly if meaning as expression and perception is contingent upon cultural forms, there is a relation here that requires our attention. For the relation constitutes the capabilities and limitations of human culture itself. The specialists who address meaning via its own "science" have insisted, more or less eclectically, that meaning is an effect of signs—abstract codings or functions that can be used to rationalize the whole matter as some sort of epiphenomenal order.

This assumed, or working, definition has the effect of mak-

ing meaning subordinate to signs, and it makes studies of
meaning into exercises in semiology or semiotics, a science of
signs and their orderings. I argue that such an approach is apt
to constrain the meaning of naming things within the naming
of meanings, that is, to reflect inadvertently the convention-
alism and rationality of scholarly procedure within the subject
of study. I argue, therefore, in *The Invention of Culture,* that the
interpretive elicitation of meanings, which I call "invention,"
can be seen to have a life of its own, and can mold the use of
cultural conventions to its purposes. It is, in fact, locked into
a dialectical relation with cultural convention, and we must
look to this dialectic if we are fully to comprehend human
expression and cultural motivation.

For many readers of *The Invention of Culture,* this may have
seemed an unwarranted assumption—too close, perhaps, to
assuming that meaning is a "black box" and a free-floating
intangible. That the dialectic of invention and convention is a
plausible ground for cultural meaning and motivation, that it
grounds, and is grounded in, the treatment of the individual
and the collective, may be clear enough to perceptive readers
of that volume. That these operations can be extrapolated to
larger issues of culture is also a part of that message. Unless
demonstrated, however, such an extension may seem something of an unwarranted assumption.

This is, perhaps, a familiar dilemma to many who have
accepted the elicitative nature of trope; as metaphor, metonym,
or whatnot, it elicits meaning. But as long as the elicitation is
a function of local, or epigrammatic expressions alone, rather
than an overall, organizing effect, culture becomes a fabric of
tropes stitched together by conventional "structure," categories, and other conventionalizing devices. If we are to come to
terms with the implications of meaning for culture as a phenomenon, then, it is necessary to show how trope itself can
operate as an organizing principle.

But the nature of trope makes this a formidable problem at
best. For trope—as metaphor, metonym, or whatever—is in
essence unglossable and paradoxical. To show how trope organizes culture is to show how paradox does, and paradox has

functioned in modern life, in literary image, camp, Zen, counterculture, merely as a means of *stopping* conventional procedures, jolting them into self-consciousness. Organization must surely be made of sterner stuff. One can, after all, groove on the delicious ironies of metaphor until one's herb tea boils over, or be driven punchdrunk by the ambitious pummeling of Zen masters without the *koan* ever being jolted into a *satori* that changes one's life. Irony, however precious it might be, is not explanation, and it is not explication.

The strategy of this book is to show, with examples taken from my research in New Guinea, and from the articulation of "core" symbols in Western history, how the essentially paradoxical effect of trope expands from a play on conventional "points of reference" into an organizer of cultural frames. Indeed, it expands beyond that level into what I shall call higher "powers" of trope, eventually closing upon itself to constitute its own ground conditions—the individuality of perception and the plurality of collective "embodiment."

The holography that retains the properties of trope throughout this expansion is best exemplified through the recursive processual form that I have called *obviation*. Obviation is manifested as a series of substitutive metaphors that constitute the plot of a myth (or the form of a ritual), in a dialectical movement that closes when it returns to its beginning point. A myth, then, is an expansion of trope, and obviation, as process, is paradoxical because the meanings elicited in its successive tropes are realized only in the process of their exhaustion, and exhausted in that of their realization.

The order and referentiality of language and the iconicity of personal perception can never, in themselves, be absolute determinants of meaning, for we know each of them only through the mediation of the other. Overprecision in defining them as "functions," or methodologizing them, lends an air of professionalism, but only that, to our understanding of meaning. Meaning is constituted in the *limen* between word and full, perceptual image, and I have used a "metaformat" of diagrams that are intermediate between abstraction and representational image to illustrate the obviative process. But their "triangulation" is no more "structure" than it *is* obviation; it is a navigational aid, if you will, to catch the parallax of meaning as it moves beyond our ken.

The approach I have taken in this book is "dialectical" (rather than "algorithmic") in the mathematical sense, meaning that it deals with constitutive or "existential" conditions of its subject, rather than with causal chains or the arbitration among alternative descriptive glosses. The "bracketing," or elicitation, of an issue *contains* the issue in many possible or alternative ways, but is a very different concern from the "truth value," or propositional status, of the issue. Thus evidence is largely a concern with illustrating, or exemplifying (rather than "proving") the model suggested. The evidential materials I have used come from a broad and disparate cross-section of the literature: material that I collected among the Daribi people of Papua New Guinea, Nancy Munn's iconographic studies of the Walbiri of Australia, discussions of Western time concepts and technology, an overview of some historical topics relevant to the "core" symbolizations of medieval religious, and modern secular philosophy, and finally, some evolutionary issues involving the human brain and body.

An earlier form of chapter 4 was read at Brown University in September, 1983, and the discussion following that occasion was in many respects germinal to the final version. I am grateful especially to Lina Fruzzetti, Akos Östör, and Harriet Whitehead for their insightfulness. Many other friends have helped, in one way or another, to elicit or focus these ideas, among them especially Victor Turner, Stanley Walens, Fitz-John Porter Poole, Marilyn Strathern, James F. Weiner, and John Napora, deserve my thanks. Finally, I am more grateful than I can say to those whose efforts have been *constitutive* of this book: to David M. Schneider, a mentor whose encouragement, concern, and support approach the point of devotion; to Mary Alice Carter, the sun goddess of this work; and to my "Antonie Brentano," Nancy-Sue Ammerman.

1 Introduction

What are symbols, that we should be concerned with them? They are certainly not something that "the natives" have told the anthropologist about, though natives are often outspoken about what we call their "content." Rather, it seems, they are something that we often say the natives themselves are all about. Are symbols, then, a kind of a disease of civilization, that we in our ministrations, like so many Typhoid Marys, unwittingly communicate to the natives? Or, conversely, is civilization itself a disease of symbols, as Max Muller suggested that myth is a disease of language? The more visible product of the fieldworker's interaction has to do with language, and the possibility that the social sciences with their involuted jargons are themselves a disease of language is an issue that has sometimes been raised by third-world skeptics. ("Mystification" is the trendy epithet.) But language, they say, is something we know all about; it is ultimately symbolic. So, we have learned, is money. And so we return to the original question. Are symbols the academic currency, a coinage minted by the postcolonial knowledge industries so that, drawing upon an immense capital of accumulated literatures, philosophies, and established "facts," we can buy up the semantic production of all-too-aptly named research "subjects"? Money, so long as it is our money, is the only trade item the would-be entrepreneur need gift the natives with; the rest takes care of itself, for the house never loses.

Granting that this might be so, is it really a time for new coinages, reevaluated and reissued denominations that will bring out the "true" value of money by making its orders, and perhaps even its diseases, more explicit? Do we need a currency of inflation? Perhaps in economics, for this is an old trick of the Caesars, of old civilizations gone to pawn. If credibility is not saved, as least its demise is stalled off by making people count things all over again. (And the house never loses.) But it will not help the currency of symbols, for generating new denominations of semiotic functioning merely compounds the interest on the debt, making the denomination of problems a function of the problem of denomination.

In his study of modern narcissism, *The Fall of Public Man,* Richard Sennett relates the "inflation" to social norms:

> We speak of symbols having 'referents,' for ex-
> ample, of having 'antecedents.' The symbol easily
> loses a reality of its own in this usage: 'When
> you say that, or use that word, what you really
> mean is . . .' and so on. One of the social origins
> of the idea of decoding signs can be traced to a
> century ago, in the interpretation of appearances
> which came to be made in the 19th century city:
> appearance is a cover for the real individual hid-
> den within.[1]

Symbolic penetration and hermeneutic, the "decoding" of conventional life, is for Sennett a sociological concomitant of an age that has lost the confidence and credibility of a system of conventional public signs; social life, then, becomes symbolic when it can no longer be credibly social. If the imperial Romans can be said to have gotten the better of their disbelief by butchering real characters in fake myths before live audiences, then a society that disbelieves its own language might at least be content with veridical theories of language . . . or of symbols.

Of course symbols, and theories of symbols, are both more ancient and more modern than the nineteenth-century city; what Sennett's example suggests is a reason why symbols are emphasized in contemporary life. That symbols should be seen as cryptic, and problematic, that interpretation is a necessary

---

1. Richard Sennett, *The Fall of Public Man* (New York: Alfred A. Knopf, 1977), 79.

adjunct to analysis, that the crucial underpinnings and workings of meaning and human culture are somehow involved in
symbols, or semantics, or semiotics, is a central preoccupation
of our times. The expectations and contingencies of this issue
lie at the root of philosophical undertakings from Wittgenstein
and Husserl to Sartre and Ricoeur, and they are basic to what
has been called "symbolic anthropology." But it is also significant that the vain and precocious medieval rhetorician
Berengar of Tours insisted, to the amazement and dismay of
his peers, that the Holy Sacrament was but a symbol, and that
something rather like structuralism—the "method" of Pierre
de La Ramée[2]—dominated the intellectual life of pre-Enlight-
enment Europe. Like money, and like God, symbols were always there.

It is really what we make of them that counts. If God, for
Ramée, perhaps, no less than for Berengar, was somehow mysteriously *behind* things, ethereal and working in wondrous
ways, then for modern Westerners money, and symbols too,
are somehow mysteriously *in front* of things, too elemental for
easy or ordinary comprehension. Marxism, economics, and also
semiotics, belong to a mysticism of the exoteric.

Our everyday world takes points of reference for granted,
and the expectations and values that those points of reference
set up—precision, accountability, predictability, consistency,
and the like—frame theories for the meanings that lie "behind"
them. Understanding "point" as an elemental unit, a phoneme,
lexeme, spoken or written symbol, and "reference" in the
double-edged sense of being both a fixed token of common
orientation and something that signifies by referring to something else, our concern for meaning becomes a science of meaning—usually a linguistics of meaning.[3] Like produce in general,

2. Walter J. Ong, *Ramus: Method and the Decay of Dialogue* (Cambridge,
Mass.: Harvard University Press, 1958).

3. Were semantics and semiotics truly experimental sciences, like quantum
physics, they would soon find themselves adducing paradoxical properties to
signs and functions (moving "backward in time" like the positron, containing
entire supernumerary "dimensions," like some small particles, modeling geo-
metrical properties, like the graviton). These functions and properties are par-

meaning is *assigned* a value, and epistemology becomes the (scientific) problem of how that value operates. (In this regard modern civilization, with its overconfident value assignments, brings its own social sciences upon itself.)

What becomes provocative for an intellectual enterprise constituted along these lines is the degree to which meaning is *not* an economy of symbols, or of systems, as of course evolution may not be DNA Sweepstakes, or physics a game of underwriting the insurance of very small particles. Units, elements, combinatory systems, and periodic tables give a nice feeling for dealing with the phenomenal universe in the precise, accountable, predictable ways in which we like to think we run our own shop. And if God, to paraphrase Einstein, does not play dice with the universe, the scientist who wants to get the better of the elusive and the provocative is obliged to enter a floating crap game with definitions. How to define units—money, symbols, subatomic particles—so that they will retain credibility as points of reference (and their accountability and predictability as well) in a theoretical enterprise? Failing that, how to define, or frame, any viable alternative?

Structuralism gets the better of this impasse by making definitions (verbal, systematic oppositions) themselves the units; astute humanistic critiques and semiotics do so with characterizations (and with the metaphors that, according to Paul Ricoeur, are all that can do justice to other metaphors). Points of reference are not determinative, but only necessary, as money becomes so—contingently—necessary that it is printed on paper, then in books, and then becomes a vending-machine function of integers. A game of redefinition that maneuvers so adeptly about points of reference must come home, as did Einstein's field theory, to roost on the relativity of coordinate systems. We come down, eventually, to the self-referential symbol, the trope or metaphor, as a beginning point for a discussion of meaning.

---

adoxical because they reference the implications of an imagery that is disallowed by the defining conditions of sign or particle. Quantum physics misses the *scale* of human experience, and must compensate for it; linguistic approaches to meaning miss the scale of the world in which meaning operates.

Metaphor, the symbol whose gloss is definitively relative, is the perfect and appropriate point of reference for an age of cryptic symbols and inscrutable meanings; its "discovery" by every critical, scientific, and aesthetic enterprise concerned with meaning is inevitable. It is our own mirror image, and we, perhaps, are its. The very ambitious attempt to grammaticize it, the humanistic adumbrate its character, and psychologists run rats through it. As with God and money, and symbols in general for that matter, it is what we make of it that counts. If it reflects the linguist's ambition to resolve everything into rule and order, the wonder and admiration of aesthetes and literati, the psychologist's scientistic interrogative, how can it be made to model the complexity of meaning known to the anthropologist?

Cultural relativity, like Einstein's, is often no more than the relativity of coordinate (or reference) systems, of language, ethos, acquired "feel," and habit. To know it, experience it, one gets used to living somewhere else, with "other" people. This is an introduction to the issue. But trope or metaphor, the self-referential coordinate, is relativity compounded; it introduces relativity *within* coordinate systems, and within culture. Thus expressions within a culture are relative to, innovative upon, and ambiguous with regard to, one another. A model founded upon these relations is, if it is systematic at all, a mobile, fluid, and an undetermined system.

Like the black hole (which also has, in the jargon of astrophysicists, "no hair"—by which it might be grasped), the effects of metaphor have been listed, analyzed, tallied, even synthesized through metaphors, to an exhaustive degree. A great many of the "positions" taken on metaphor are quite accurate and insightful,[4] though one suspects that a "complete" characterization would be as unattainable, and as useless, as the "complete" glossing of a single metaphor. Possibly also the

---

4. The idea that metaphor has "emergent" or transcendental qualities is by no means uncommon. Paul Ricoeur speaks of the power of metaphoric utterance to "redescribe a reality inaccessible to direct description" (*Time and Narrative,* trans. K. McLaughlin and D. Pellbauer [Chicago: University of Chicago Press, 1984], xl).

"correct" characterization of metaphor is as much a chimera as the correct glossing of one. It would seem, however, that what one can do, analytically, with metaphor is more important than what metaphor "does."

A summary, or review of the "state of the art" regarding metaphor might possibly help here, for all that my discussion is not aimed at literary criticism, or at the state of anyone's art, and is not "about" metaphor. But I shall limit my brief digression to a few essentials, and expand on these subsequently.

A metaphor, and, by extension, a trope generally, equates one conventional point of reference with another, or substitutes one for another, and obliges the interpreter to draw his or her conclusions as to the consequences. It elicits analogies, as perceptions *through* language, so to speak, and these analogies or perceptions become the intent, and the content, of the expression.

Figurative usage, then, because it makes a kind of prism of conventional reference, cannot provide a literal field of reference. It is not formed by "indicating" things, or by referencing them, but by setting pointers or reference points into a relation with one another, by making them into a relation that is innovative upon the original order of reference. It "conveys" a renegotiated relation, but, not being "literal" in any sense, cannot "point" to it. Thus we may say that it "embodies" or "images" its object, figuring sympathetically by becoming itself that which it expresses. When we speak of things that do not have conventional referents, then our manner of speaking must itself become the referent. The effect of the construction is embodied in its impingement upon conventional reference; this impingement is simultaneously what it *is,* and what it is *about.*

An autistic symbol, a symbol that stands for itself, is not so much an impossibility as an inanity—who cares? Such a construct is interesting, and relevant to anyone's concern, only insofar as it touches upon—converts, inverts, reverts, subverts, perverts—and as it *relates* to, conventional points of reference. It concerns us as *relatively* self-contained, self-significative. Metaphors may indeed be the jewels of prose and poetry, the death-clear lakes of reflection and alienation that star the mountain ranges of Shakespeare, Goethe, and Federico García Lorca, they may indeed run the gamut of modern existential ambivalence from everything to nothing, but they are significant for the anthropological modeling of culture, and that is what concerns me here—not in how they embellish, but how they constitute, culture.

What have we learned of this constitution thus far? It is clear that a culture compounded of *relative* meanings cannot be a system of oppositions, as the structuralists would have it, for relativity implies a move to new coordinates that denies, or negates, the original ones. Innovative meanings are emergent—they preempt one another, and draw force and credibility from one another. Culture is but analogy based on (and subversive to) other analogies, not in a tension of rigid oppositions or categories, but a mobile range of transformations worked upon a conventional core.

But that core is itself a kind of residue, "conventional" only because some particular set, or combination, of its analogic associations has been identified as the most literal, or common—a definitional "absolute." A set of cultural reference points so identified—the rules and lexicon of a language, for instance—amount to a universal, basic metaphor that provides us with the facility of being literal. Because they are parts or facets (in fact, metonyms) of the framing metaphor, words, mathematical expressions, and other statements have a conventional reference; they are taken in the context, so to speak, of the larger, framing metaphor.

And of course it is true that a language, or mathematics, has internal imageries within its grammar, syntax, and usage that constitute a frame within a frame, what we might wish to call "imageries of convention." In French, one would say "the moon, she is a lovely woman," but in German it would have to be "the moon, *he* is a lovely woman," and in the Daribi language of New Guinea it would be *sugua ge ware we meniraba'*—"the moon pearlshell a fine woman, as it were." In these differences the framing metaphors become apparent as such, and lend subtle ironies of their own to the "translatability" of figurative expression. In mathematics, one would have to say that i, the square root of -1, is a metaphor, since it registers an impasse in the calculibility of the terms used, and, because it is therefore "imaginary," it comes to stand for an imaginary realm or field.

The conventions—rules, syntax, lexicon—of language stand in a reciprocal relation to that which can be, and is, said in the language. As we speak by working transformations upon those conventions, *figuring* our meanings through them, so the set of conventions can be seen as the metaphor of all that could be said in this way. A language, and, insofar as it can be said to have conventions (which is how we, perforce, describe it), a culture, is the ultimate subjunctive, an "as if" made into an "is" by the seriousness of those who use it.

Once we admit this, that the ostensibly "positive" or "absolute" values are not in themselves absolute, but relative figures that are manipulated by framing the lesser, more obvious ones within the larger, more conventional ones, then it becomes apparent that expression is not only relative *between* languages, but also *within* them. Formal language then becomes the increment of a game in which lesser figures are formed within and against the larger, framing ones, and eventually become encapsulated by them, only to facilitate the formation of yet other, lesser expressions.

The formal side of expression is, of course, not only a factor in verbal and conceptual articulation, but a polarity in the realm of perception as well, with implications that I shall consider presently. (Relative abstraction or concreteness is simply another dimension in which the reciprocal relationship among frames occurs; it makes "concrete" and "abstract" metaphors of one another.) The "absolute" nature of such frames belongs to a conventionalist, or literalist perspective, one that would have to, at this juncture, figuratively cut the human *corpus callosum*. Unmediated concrete and abstract thought, a truly "split" brain, the hierarchical logical "types" of Russell and Whitehead, or the codes, axes, and matrices of the structuralist, give us our cultural and contextual frames ready-made. Convenient, in that they do not require explanation, they are also arbitrary—making order absolute for the sake of order itself.

The alternative approach, and the task of this discussion, is to show how this framing occurs as a consequence of meaningful construction—how the frames are invented out of one another, so to speak. Specifically, as I have selected the trope, or metaphor, as the unit of self-reference, the task is to demonstrate how a metaphor expands the frame of its self-referentiality by processual extension into a broader range of cultural relevance—a larger frame, and a larger metaphor. A trope is no longer necessarily an instantaneous flash, but potential process, and its process—the constituting of cultural frames—is simultaneously also revelation, or knowledge process.

A relative perspective *within* the province of cultural construction, taking the referentialism of the symbol, the "is" of convention, as a kind of subjunctive, is to enter a tentative suspension—Vaihinger's world of "as if."[5] Instead of a "system" of categories, axes, institutions—conventional points of reference made into steel girders—we have points of reference rather like notes in a musical score. Always "there" in potential, as components of the scales known, if only intuitively, to composer, performer, and listener, the notes take on a meaning according to the themes, variations, harmonies, and sonorities of the music itself. And if it is meaning we would study, then the meaning is in the music, and only contingently in its possibilities.

Especially since this all sounds like structuralism without structure, *bricolage* as the essence of culture, we have to ask what *use* this all is. Why *not* take symbols as units at face value, guaranteed by the federal reserve system that D. Sperber calls "encyclopedic knowledge,"[6] and use this capital to make shrewd investments in the world of ethnological production?

5. Hans Vaihinger, *The Philosophy of As If: A System of the Theoretical, Practical, and Religious Fictions of Mankind,* trans. G. K. Ogden (London: Routledge & Kegan Paul, 1968).

6. Dan Sperber, *Rethinking Symbolism,* trans. A.L. Morton (Cambridge: Cambridge University Pres, 1975).

Structure has the credibility of product, symbol the potency of money, whereas metaphor has all the credibility and potency of . . . daydream.

The answer lies not, of course, in any poetry or precision that metaphor might bring to ethnology—turning kinship and ritual into literature, and us into literary critics. It inheres, rather, in the possibility that trope as symbol and symbol as trope might be mutually reinforcing; that the significance and the workings of trope might be rendered more coherent by modeling cultural construction upon it, spreading it out across the cultural spectrum.

The process of modeling in science, and in social science, makes use of known, familiar relations or orderings as a basis for the analogic comprehension of some heretofore unorganized material. A metaphor is made, and expanded into a perception within the properties of the material to be grasped, so that the idea of a double helix or of floating tectonic plates, for instance, is "seen" to inform the structure of DNA, or the motility of the earth's crust. The "seeing" itself is "new" knowledge, and because a metaphor is self-significative, the knowledge acquires a galvanizing force from its apparent (and de facto) uniting of knower and known—hence the certainty that carries scientific paradigms. And the consequences of such a confident "seeing" include a restructuring of the model, the heretofore familiar, by the research material: DNA becomes a model for the double-helical, geography for the floating and flowing of solids.

To use the modeling procedure itself as a model for culture is to adduce "paradigm certainty" for cultural motivation in general, for the invention of culture. But it is also to take a second-order derivative—the modeling of modeling is modeling. And so our choice of the model to be used becomes important. If we choose scientific methodology and modeling as the field of "known and familiar relations and orderings," then culture emerges, as for the ethnomethodologists, as the folk science of doing life. If we choose the received knowledge concerning signs and semiotics, semantics and pragmatics, as a model, then culture becomes an electrical display of scholarly definitions, a particle physics of icons encapsulating referents, frame markers marking frames—functions (or namings) that stand for themselves. And if we choose the piquant metaphors by which insightful literary (or literary/social/semiotic) critics have characterized and dramatized metaphor, then culture is, perhaps, a dancing text, dazzling, concealing, revealing, possibly psychoanalyzing its readers or participants.

An alternative is to wager the open, nescient, "black-hole" qualities (or nonqualities) of metaphor, as model, against its own expansion into myth or ritual, modeling ethnography on metaphor, and metaphor upon ethnography, in the hope that the known unfamiliar and the unknown familiar may help to structure one another. If we assume that kinship, or myth, or ritual, to take three of the anthropologist's favorite generalities, is, in its working out, the sequential construction of a metaphor, a cultural trope in large, expanded frames, then we will, in effect, view the mechanism of the metaphor and its glossing. If we pay attention to the logic, or sequencing of things, we might also gather some evidence as to the staging of a gloss, its ethnography, so to speak, what meaning makes people do.

A metaphor is at once proposition and resolution; it stands for itself. Expanded outward to encompass (and define) the larger cultural frames, the self-definition and the pull toward resolution lend their force to cultural motivation and action. Meaning acquires in this way a form as well as a content, acquires a form through its content. As the form and constitution of a lexicon always bears the subtle imprint of the metaphors that can be, and have been, formed against it (B minor was never the same after Bach's Mass, C-sharp minor after Beethoven's Quartet), so the formal part of a culture accommodates, and is charged by, the large-frame myths, rituals, and kin constructions that take form out of it, and form it. And what we see as the general pattern of a culture, its galactic structure (as David Schneider would have it[7]) of core symbology, must bear the imprint of the generic form and self-closure of large-

7. David M. Schneider, "Notes toward a Theory of Culture," in K. Basso and H. Selby, eds., *Meaning in Anthropology* (Albuquerque: University of New Mexico Press, 1976).

frame metaphors or tropes. In this regard the "deep structure" of a culture is only partially mode and content, B minor and C-sharp minor; it is also what I have called obviation, with its necessary paradoxes and negations.

Myths, ritual, and kin relations, seen as expanded tropes, as cultural frames with a logic or overlay of their own, carry us, like Ruth Benedicts's "patterns" or Spenglerian "cycles," considerably beyond the anthropology of social affairs. They call up the specter of cultural determinism, or, if that sense of culture is too strong, meaning determinism, and they draw attention away from political ends, political motives, and the role of the actor within the drama. At best, metaphor and the flow of analogy that it elicits, writ large or small, can only influence the relative contingency of human actions. It deflects the substantive, the concrete "thingnesses" of things, as well as the symbols that name them as such, as it dissolves the sense of "actor" into a kind of general "sensorium" of meanings.

For this reason, then, metaphor, as I have introduced it here, portends only a very "left-handed" (or "left-sided") determinism, a relational dimension of perspective and perception that deals with bounding conditions and existential issues. The question of its scientific status could, indded, be raised, as it predicts nothing and is impervious to our cultural games of testing, controlling, and validation, but then various ethical question of its scientific status could, indeed, be raised, as it predicts nothing and is impervious to our cultural games of testing, controlling, and validation, but then various ethical questions could also be raised regarding the advisability of a usable, highly determinist social science. (Mathematics, "Queen of the Sciences," is entirely a work of the imagination, and thus one of the humanities.) Meaning is a perception in symbolic value space; trope is the elicitor and vehicle of perception. But perception itself is arguably the most potent of the human qualities: not only are our great symphonies and works of visual art essentially perceptions, but also our technology is nothing if not a corpus of detailed, consistent, pragmatic perceptions, and perception lies at the core of our deadliest weapons and our most compelling speculative triumphs.

The use of trope, and obviation, as a model allows one to speak with some confidence about generalities that more pragmatic, predictive, and strategy-oriented approaches can only try to explain away. When we speak of meaning, we are talking about "seeing" within the world of human symbols, not about the grammars, syntaxes, or sign functions through which order can be precipitated out of expression. To use the algorithms whose instrumentality is modeled on linguistic capability is one thing; to develop a facility for "reading" the flow of image-developed analogy, the dialectic of meanings, is quite another.

What, then, is the relation of perception to cultural reference point? Is it a matter of abstraction, sign, and referent, as Saussure seems to have thought? Let me turn, now, to the matter of concept and percept.

2 Too Definite for Words

There are two ways in which names, as symbols, can be considered. We can consider them as "codings," or points of reference, merely representing the things named, or we can consider them in terms of the relation between the symbol and the thing symbolized. In the first instance naming becomes matter of contrasts and grouping among the names themselves: a microcosm of symbols is deployed to code or represent the world of reference. The world of phenomena is self-evident and apart. In the second instance naming becomes a matter of analogy: symbol and symbolized belong to a single relation, a construction within a larger world, or macrocosm.

The distinction here is not a trivial one, because all words, and all symbols, insofar as they are points of reference, can be considered "namings." It is clear that both modes of viewing symbols, as coding and as analogy, have a certain potential, and that the construction of an explanatory microcosm called "structure" realizes only part of the potential. The other part involves a mode of construction that includes symbol and symbolized within the same expression, and implies, among other things, that the symbolized is no less a part of culture than the symbol.

To give an example, among the Daribi people of Papua New Guinea, the verb form *poai* (a participle of the verb *poie,* "to be named," "to be congruent with") is used to indicate the relation of a person or thing to the element for which it has been named.[1] The two, denominator and denominated, are said to be *sabi* (i.e., "tail"), or "namesakes," of one another, elements, that is, that have a (socially) recognized "as if" relationship

1. Roy Wagner, *Habu: The Innovation of Meaning in Daribi Religion,* (Chicago: University of Chicago Press, 1972), pp. 85–94.

with each other. The actual, verbal "name" is treated as a function of this relationship; thus, if a person is named for something with a plurality of conventional designations (a sulphur-crested cockatoo, for instance), all of these designations are considered equally to be names of the person (e.g., *nara, terawai*).

Such a relationship is individual, and individuating, in relation to convention, because it cancels or suspends the order of conventional reference in which men, for instance, and cockatoos are assumed to be distinct and nonoverlapping entities. The "as if" of the name, so to speak, sets itself in opposition to the "as if" of referential designation; the name defines for itself a possibility, excluded by convention, in which a man might be considered, for whatever reason, to be similar to, and thus "be," a cockatoo. That possibility coincides rather uniquely with the name, and so we may conclude that the name "stands for" the possibility that it elicits (and hence signifies its own relationship, or itself),[2] and also that it self-references itself through that possibility. To call a man "Sulphur-crested Cockatoo" is to give the man an individuality insofar as a metaphor of his being a cockatoo is allowed. But the "as if" of this possibility must necessarily impinge upon the "as if" of the collective referential, or "coding" systems, primarily because they both use the same set of conventions. Thus the symbols are used again and again, entering into varying combinations, and it is the self-referencing possibilities of the constructs that change and differentiate themselves, creating the collective as an innovation upon the individual, and vice versa.

If we treat names as merely names, points of reference, then symbolism becomes a matter of reference: a microcosm of names is counterposed to a macrocosm of referents. But if we treat "name" as relationship, the microcosm of names is no longer a microcosm; it becomes immersed in a macrocosm of analogic construction. Not only do we have an analogy that encompasses name and named, but that analogy suggests, and

2. This position recalls the "possible worlds" argument that Kripke uses against the Frege-Russell notion of the descriptive nature of naming. See Saul A. Kripke, *Naming and Necessity*, (Cambridge, Mass.: Harvard University Press, 1980), 48–60.

tends to enter us into, analogic relations among macrocosmic constructs.

The participle *poai* indicates *any* resemblance that can be found between some person or thing (or state, act, or whatever) and another. People who share one point of resemblance (and a name itself is a point of resemblance, however it may have been acquired) share all of their resemblances, for *poai* names them "the same." On this basis, all people have an infinite range of "names," all are in some sense "named" all things, and all of these names and people are one. (The one name, incidentally, is *poai*, "named," which an otherwise nonplussed Daribi parent can bestow in recognition of the child's just having been named—"*poai*"; the alternative is to name it, using the negative infix, for its recent unnamed state—*poʒiawai*, "unnamed." Both names are common.) The problem is more one of stopping, or conventionalizing, the flow of analogies—the "pull" from one analogy to all others—than of finding analogies. The name (or names) that is *socially* recognized serves to mediate among personal resemblances so as to control the analogic flow for social purposes. If a name is a social point of reference, an individuating relationship, then it is so because it artificially *stops* the flow at the point of that relationship. Thus the microcosm of social names *mediates* the macrocosm of analogy by cutting it into manageable pieces. And the macrocosm of analogy, of course, mediates the microcosmic points of reference by allowing us to "see" resemblances among them, bridging them into *sabi* relationships among people, or people and animals (fig. 1). Daribi say that *sabi* should help one another.

If names are symbols, and symbols names, it should be no trouble to make this special case of naming a general case of symbolism. All we need to do is expand the sense of "name" into an instance of microcosmic restriction, and the sense of *poai*, analogy, into the range of all perceptual phenomena that form, or that may form, the basis for human experience and communication. We can then confront, on a more cosmic basis, the issue of symbolism, and we can also deal with the mediation that serves to negotiate human cultural conception and action within it. (And if we reflect on the fact that mediation actually creates the analogies and codings, by the simple fact of negotiating them, it emerges that "negotiating" human cultural conception and action is the same as creating, or inventing, it.)

Perception has characteristically been treated as a kind of natural function in studies of meaning, a phenomenal realm serving as a frontier area of meaning, from which symbolism takes its expressive media, and upon which it imposes (as in

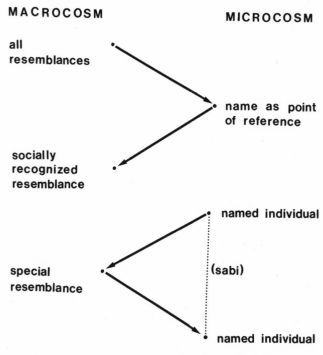

FIGURE 1: Mediation in Daribi naming practice.

"apperception") an order and an orientation. The Saussurian notion of the "sign" as a sensual mediator between concept and percept (as well as other similar ideas, such as that of the phoneme, or the musical tone) is itself a "sign" of this assumptional framework, which centers the crucial areas of meaning upon symbolic points of reference, their grammars, syntaxes, and so forth. Recent studies in neurophysiology suggest, however, that perception is more than a frontier of symbolism with the natural world—that it is, in fact, centrally involved.

Bela Julesz, of Bell Telephone Laboratories, speaks of "cyclopean perception"—that which results in the "formation of a percept at some central location in the visual system by using stimuli that could not possibly produce that percept at an earlier location."[3] The most familiar example of such "global" information, as Julesz would have it, is that of stereoscopic vision, which is based on "peripheral" information from the two optical retinas, but which would require a special, internal "retina" for the formation of the image. He cites experimental evidence to indicate that meaning in visual art, music, poetry, and linguistic expression generally is "cyclopean" in this sense,[4] and notes that

> the cyclopean mind is a giant since the great majority of all the neural input of our nervous system enters into it. It is also a simpleton, incapable of the symbolic manipulations so essential in languages, logic, and mathematics; and it lacks the ability of abstraction.[5]

Meaning, it seems, is itself a perception, and its experiencing and expression are oblique to the ordering of grammars and points of reference, which are, at best, its elicitors. More than this, meaning is a perception *within* what we could call the "value space" set up by symbolic points of reference, a "stereoscopic" view, if you will, of different symbolic points of reference brought to focus at a single cyclopean "retina." It is thus the perception of analogy, and its expansion into larger forms, or frames, of culture takes the form of a "flow" of analogy.

The identification of the sign as a mediator between percept and symbolic concept establishes *abstraction*—the birth of order

3. Bela Julesz, *Foundations of Cyclopean Perception,* (Chicago: University of Chicago Press, 1971), 3.

4. Ibid., 53.

5. Ibid., 14.

as accomplished fact—as the single constitutive act in the emergence of meaning. Forever after speculation has been aroused as to the origin of language, the invention of abstraction that formed the Word in the Beginning. But the realization that meaning *is* perception, occurring within the "natural" ground from which abstraction supposedly freed the word, indicates that "abstraction" is, rather, part of a generative and ongoing process. The invention of a microcosm by abstraction from a perceptual macrocosm is half of a highly charged dialectical interaction, establishing a sensory continuum within which the ordering and refiguring of meaning is accomplished. The other half of this charged interaction is an equally significant expansion, or concretization, of microcosm into macrocosm that occurs in the formation of analogy. The invention of microcosm, of symbol and language, and of macrocosm, meaning and meaningful world, are intrinsically and dialectically related aspects of the same process.

The coding of microcosms, sensorily and qualitatively restricted media for the representation of symbolic reference, seems to be universal in human cultures. Spoken language is the most obvious, and perhaps the most important, instance, though nonverbal "body languages" and inscribed, visual codings also furnish examples. Such codes are invariably generated through a limitation and restriction of sensory range, a diminished background against which minute variations, such as minor sound inflections or the shapes of letters or numbers, can be used to represent significant points of variation. Restriction of this sort determines a kind of redundancy, often remarked upon by theorists of language, in which what are recognizably the same sounds or images keep recurring in the course of expression. The recurrence actually makes use of the coding medium, the sensual component of symbolization, to convey a sense (in large part illusory) of referential invariance; a given sound or orthographic symbol marks the "point" for a point of reference. As the point holds its place, so does the reference.

In considering the realization of the microcosm, I should like to draw upon the particularly felicitous example provided by Professor Nancy D. Munn, in her studies of iconographic representation among the Walbiri people of central Australia.[6] Like the graphic representations of other central desert peoples, notably, for instance, the Arunta, Walbiri iconographs stand in a profound relation to the cosmological and ritual realizations of the traditional life.

While they most certainly describe a microcosm, the ambiguities inherent in their representative mode disqualify them from consideration as "written language" in the conventional sense of discursive phonography or ideography.

It could well be argued, on the other hand, that for all their divergence from the mimesis of speech characteristic of a phonographic script such as our own, such iconographs do approximate the ideography of traditional Chinese and Japanese writing. There are, of course, far fewer "characters" than we find in the Oriental orthographies, but here again the possibility arises that the ambiguities of the Australian codes are not necessarily more formidable, but merely differently situated. For they are stylized and abstracted pictures, not of sounds or ideas, but of the impressions that are (or would be) made in the earth by beings that move across it, or of static forms situated upon the earth. Many of the most commonly used forms are in fact close imitations of the tracks of human beings or animals.

A juxtaposition of the graphs is always readable as a sort of abstract diagram or map, provided that the context is clearly understood (a more literally inclined tradition would doubtless devise "sense signs," like those furnished in ancient Egyptian hieroglyphics, for this purpose). The iconographs are inscribed in areas of loose sand in accompaniment to ordinary conversation as well as to illustrate a women's narrative that Munn calls the "sand story."[7] In these cases their continuity seems to be a more or less ideographic one, following the episodes of the narration or conversation. The cosmologically significant depictions made and used by men, however, generally base their continuity on that of the track, or route, of a person or

6. Nancy D. Munn, *Walbiri Iconography: Graphic Representation and Cultural Symbolism in a Central Australian Society,* (Ithaca: Cornell University Press, 1973).
7. Ibid., 59.

being moving across the country. A track can be *followed* (*bura*[8]) in its creation or interpretation, and movement "along" the spatial progression that is graphically depicted or implicit in the "line" of songs sung about successive points or episodes in the journey has the effect of modeling the continuity of spoken discourse upon a spatial traverse.

The country of these people is, of course, known and experienced through the known trails and landmarks that such continuities represent. Indeed, since the traditional Walbiri must perforce, as hunters and gatherers, not only gain their living by following tracks (in hunting), but also spend their lives constantly *making* tracks themselves, that life in all of its acts became a process of *inscription*. And this inscription, in large part an endless repetition of domestic and productive acts, a "following" of custom and technique, was also a retracing of trails and tracks that had been known from time immemorial. The life of a person is the sum of his tracks, the total inscription of his movements, something that can be traced out along the ground.

And the life course of a people, the totality of their ways, conventions, and conventionally encountered situations, is the sum of its "tracks," the trails over its country along which experience is measured out.

It is in this sense that the analogic capabilities of the "track" iconograph render it the perfect "shifter," or hinge element, between the microcosm of restricted, value-coding sensory range, and the *realization* of that microcosm in the larger world of contrastingly fuller sensory range. For a track represents itself as microcosm, as being and movement compressed onto a two-dimensional plane, and it thereby implies the fuller embodiment of this being and movement, as that which made the track. To "follow" the track is to infuse a microcosm with the existence and motion of its maker, and, by a certain analogy, any sensory enrichment of its iconography constitutes a similar reversal of the process of abstraction. To perform these operations upon the collective, summative sense of "track," as the

8. Ibid., 131.

total lifeway and experience of a people, is to realize and vivify the making of that track as a creative act.

The Walbiri, according to Munn,[9] call tracks in the sense of marks left by ancestral beings in the country *guruwari,* a term that may also be used in the abstract sense of ancestral powers embodied in the country. Like the *churinga* of the Arunta, artifacts of the creative times that contain the spirits of the creative beings,[10] *guruwari* can be used to ritually replicate or reconstitute those times. It is significant for our interest that the ritual reconstruction invariably involves a "following" of the track in some form or other, and usually a sensory enrichment of the *guruwari* as design—in the visitation of secret sites that contain such designs, or the preparation of a ground painting called a "dreaming,"[11] or through the broadening of the sound spectrum as song. Thus a constructive or creative act performed upon the *guruwari,* the sensory enrichment provided by the Walbiri themselves, takes on the sacramental sense of a communion with, or a realization of *djugurba,* the creative or "story" times ("dreamtime").

Rather than regarding such ritual syntheses or constructions as a "reversal" of the actions of creative beings, moving back from the artifact to the actions that made it, Walbiri thought regards the sensory realization of *djugurba* as following upon the precedent of the original creative acts, themselves a form of premeditated construction:

> Men gave the standard explanation that in ancestral times ancestors dreamed their songs and designs while sleeping in camp. As one informant put it: 'he dreamt his track.' On getting up, the ancestor 'put' (*yira-ni*) his designs (that is, he painted them or otherwise gave them material form) and sang his songs. As he traveled along,

9. Ibid., 119.

10. Baldwin Spencer and F.J. Gillen, *The Native Tribes of Central Australia* (New York: Dover Publications, 1968), 123.

11. Geoff Bardon, *Aboriginal Art of the Western Desert* (Adelaide: Rigby Limited, 1979), 146.

> he sang his journey . . . he sang *of* his journey, the
> events along the way.[12]

Thus the synthesis of *djugurba* is not simply the mystification of human constitutive acts (as, for instance, in a "scientific" reconstruction), but the assumption of a creativity intrinsic to the action of the creative times.

If we reflect upon the fact that the only knowledge or experience that Walbiri have, or can have, of the creative phase of the world, *djugurba,* comes about in one way or another through the human realization of microcosmic symbols expanded into myths, songs, designs, and "country," it becomes apparent that Walbiri religious life is constituted in this way. Munn comments:

> Songs are in a sense symbols or oral language,
> and ancestral design are symbols of visual or
> graphic 'language.' The ancestors are in effect
> 'talking about' the things that happen to them in
> both visual-graphic and verbal ways, and such
> 'talking' objectivates the world around them, giv-
> ing it social, communicable reality.[13]

Although it is clearly elucidated by their marvelously direct, recursive usages and epistemology, the dialectic between microcosmic codings and sensorily rich aesthetic productions is by no means limited to the Walbiri, or to central desert aborigines. It is, rather, the condition of human symbolism; a polarity or contrast opposing an artificially restricted symbolic coding to an (equally) artificially expanded iconic imagery. For the act of sensual and qualitative restriction necessary to the constitution of referential value both implies and renders possible a reflexive sensual and qualitative expansion; neither is more primary or more "natural" than the other, for both are effects of the same scission, and each realizes it character in contrast to the other.

Neither sensual restriction nor the sense of referential value

12. Munn, *Walbiri Iconography,* 146.
13. Ibid., 149.

that it facilitates is equivalent, of course, to meaning, though
the perception that we understand as "meaning" would be
inconceivable and inexpressible without symbolic reference.
Meaning requires a forged absolute, as a kind of epistemolog-
ical "lie," in order to frame such truths as it is able to convey.
By the same token perception is by no means equivalent to the
aesthetic productions through which the expansion of sensory
range is realized, yet is is bound to them, and schooled by
them, as its focus. To speak of perception without this focus is
like speaking of meaning without the orienting axes of symbolic reference. It follows from this that there is a development
of perceptual or analogic focus coincident with every symbolic
regime.

Instead of Saussure's "absolute" unit of sensual abstraction,
the sign, as a mediator between "natural" percept and the abstract coding of reference, I have suggested that a modulation
of (relative) sensory amplitude—restriction as against expansion—embodies and enacts the mediation between referential
coding and perceptual image. Referential symbolism occupies
one pole—that of coding through sensory restriction—of the
mediation, and perceptual image or analogy—self-significative
symbolism—occupies the other. Neither is more "natural" or
"cultural," more or less "artificial," than the other, and although
the dialectic as a whole can be seen as a mediative process, the
elements that it mediates are not those of nature and culture.

The mediative significance of the dialectic is best understood
by considering each of its poles as a point of mediation between
the other and an element external to the dialectic (fig. 2). The
mediation is in fact dual and recursive, negotiating the "external" polarity mediated by the dialectic within the dialectic itself.
(The dialectic, in other words, is itself a representational microcosm in relation to an "external" macrocosm.) Symbolic
codings or points of reference thus mediate between the (external) social collectivity and perceptual image, simultaneously
providing a sensory medium for the coding of referential "invariance" and conventional reference points for the orientation
and recognition of images. Perceptual images, or analogies,
mediate between the individuative, factual world and symbolic
reference, incidentalizing the referential as self-signification,

and referencing the incidental as perception through a symbolic value space.

The dialectic, then, mediates between two ideal and effectively unrealizable points, the social collectivity and concrete, individuative fact or event. No symbol ever attains complete or absolute conventionality, any more than a trope or image is ever absolutely unique. The cultural dialectic of figure 2 demarcates a range within which symbolic expressions, images, and reference points innovate upon one another as *relatively* collectivizing or differentiating. The dialectic is *enabled* by an encompassing principle of figure-ground reversal, such that

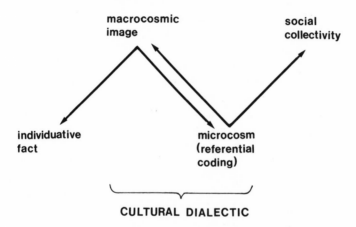

FIGURE 2: Macrocosm and microcosm as mediative foci.

each pole of the dialectic is the limiting condition of the other. An image, such as the crucified Christ in Grunewald's *Isenheim Altarpiece,* can be identified as a "symbol," and attain a certain measure of conventionality, whereas a symbolic point of reference can be seen as "back metaphor"—the "as if" of conventional usage viewed against the "is" of a metaphor formed against that usage. A symbol that stands for itself, in other words, can also stand for something else; a referential symbol can be seen to stand for itself.

Thus the cultural dialectic, the range within which the general and the particular become accessible to, and expressible

by, human beings, can, like naming, be analyzed in two different ways. It can be seen in microcosmic terms, as a semiotic
of names contrasting with names, points of reference that stand
for symbols, others that stand for their referents (or even their
reference), and still others that guarantee, like Saussure's "sign,"
the fact of abstraction itself. The result is a science of signs.
Approached from the standpoint of image rather than point,
the other alternative, however, the dialectic becomes a macrocosmic realm of embodied meanings, symbols that stand for
themselves. Such an analysis becomes, subject to the limitations inherent in image, a study of meaning. It is a "science"
to the degree that one is willing to put by predictability and
the point-precision of reference for the self-evidence of meanings that are, to paraphrase an observation of Felix Mendels-
sohn's, "too definite for words."

If macrocosmic forms may be distinguished from the microcosm through their self-signification and broadened sensory
range, they may be contrasted with (unmediated) "physical"
perception by the fact that they have significance. The significance is of course highly particularized and bound up with the
percepts themselves, rather than determined by a coding of
abstract values, But is is no less significant for all of that, and
it is certainly not the kind of simple, "natural," or primitive
significance from which australopithecines or canny high
priests once derived language by a novel act of abstraction.
And precisely because macrocosmic image is neither primitive
nor derivative, we can conclude that forms such as graphic art,
poetry, music, and ritual are not either—they must be as old,
as basic, and as important as language, for they are part of the
same condition.

The conflation of aesthetic and "everyday" images implied
in this notion of significant perception may well seem peculiar
or even erroneous in view of our tendency to consider perception a natural, and art an artificial, act. The discrimination and
recognition involved in our ordinary apprehension—seeing,
hearing, touching, and the general faculty that integrates these
"senses"—of the world around us are cultural and symbolic
activities. They are, at a very general level, every bit as cultural,
and as natural, as Mozart's composition of *The Marriage of Fi-*

garo, or as my listening to it. The realization that this is so does not render art mundane and ordinary any more than it transforms laundry lists into poetry, though it may be helpful in understanding how art can be powerful and laundry lists less so. Aesthetic images have the same symbolic valence as those of ordinary, significant perception: they belong to the dimension of self-signification. In the words of Victor Zuckerkandl:

> What tones mean musically is completely one
> with them, can only be represented through them.
> Except in the case of creative language . . .
> and of poetic language, where other, more
> 'musical' relations come into play, language
> always has a finished world of things before it,
> to which it assigns words; whereas tones must
> themselves create what they mean.[14]

The difference between ordinary perception and artistic creativity is not that between a naturalistic "sensing" of the world and an artificial, meaningful "interpretation" of that sensing, but rather it is a difference between one kind of meaningful act and another one, of greater concentration, organization, and force, within the same semiotic focus. The power of a great music, of a compelling tradition in poetry or painting, is the power of concentrating and preempting, organizing, orchestrating, and distilling, the significance that serves us in our ordinary apprehension of reality. Art is the burning glass of the sun of meaning. If this were not so, if the transcendental realizations of art were not at the same time transcendental realizations of reality, it would scarcely be necessary to disqualify aesthetic construction as mere artifice or illusion.

The point is better made by reference to the historical phenomenon of iconoclasm as it appeared in Byzantium, in Islamic culture, and among the followers of Savonarola and the English Puritans. Each of these movements was "fundamentalist" in the sense that it was commited to the status of Holy Scripture as the actual *logos,* or Word, of God or Allah. It followed from

14. Victor Zuckerkandl, *Sound and Symbol: Music and the External World,* trans. W. R. Trask, Bollingen Series XLIV (Princeton: Princeton University Press, 1969), 67.

this commitment, made emphatic often to the point of protest, that the expansion of symbolic significance into macrocosmic realization became automatically, as it were, a preempting of divine creation. Macrocosmic symbolization, in a graphically representational form, and often in other forms, such as drama, as well, was interdicted because the cultural dialectic itself had been sacralized. Where word is holy reality, its expansion is divine creation.

Another historical example, that of the French impressionists, shows that the macrocosmic nature of art can be a secular discovery as well. There is a "raising of consciousness" regarding the relationship of painting to visual "reality" that is discernible in the development of Western painting. It commenced with the invention of a "world space," continued through the awakening self-consciousness of artists who discovered brushstroke and the art of concealing art, to the crisis of "how to paint" among the artists of France and the Low Countries in the latter half of the nineteenth century. The issue was no longer, as it had been for previous centuries, the evocation of a sacred or secular world space, because the macrocosmic function of painting had been determined. The artist was in command of perception, because perception itself was something like painting; it was no longer necessary to "represent" the truer reality of the senses, but only to determine how to paint, how to use the senses to create reality. From here to the claim of the cubists, that their delineation of figures in cubical form portrayed the true reality, was but a step.

Whether it deals in cubical "realities," modulated tones, or the verbally elicited conceits of Shakespeare, art shares the qualitative (what neurophysiologists call the "spatial") symbology of perceptual experience. As a symbology the macrocosm is impervious to systemization, for the simple reason that it is already the kind of figuration that systematizing portends; to organize a percept into a system would involve a transformation or metamorphoses, and since transformation or metamorphosis is simply the means by which qualitative forms undergo change, one would merely exchange one percept for another. The problem is essentially the same as that of glossing a metaphor: the terms of the metaphor are themselves the gloss. One can, of course, discuss sensibly the impications that metaphor has for the verbal, and this is largely what our literature on metaphor involves. One can, similarly, discuss sensibly the implications of macrocosmic construction in general for cultural relations, and this is what the present study is all about.

Dealing with primitive elements that are themselves configurations, our problem is very much the opposite of the semioticist or structuralist, who seeks to determine the manifold systematics by which elemental units are combined so as to construct complexity. Appropriate transformation ("how to paint"), rather than accurate reconstruction (or deconstruction) is my goal. Like Goethe, who sought in his theories of color and plant metamorphosis to establish a natural science based on the objectivity of self-evident forms and meanings, we need to find the generic—in this case, that of cultural transformation—amid a welter of forms. Such a generic need not be a determinant, or a picture, or a structure, of "culture," but rather what we could call an image of our own "interpretation," and hence of meaning.

A single metaphor, regardless of its scope, invariably presents the enigma of what Freud called "condensation"[15]—a richness of potentially elicited analogies, all at once, that makes the "reading" of the expression, or the fixing of its intent, a matter of the interpreter's own selection. If we allow Julesz's analogy of "cyclopean" perception, then the "stereoscopic image" projected in a metaphor wants a conventional focal point. This is an intrinsic property of embodied meaning, which is always its own focal point, a point that only in some cases— the limiting cases where macrocosmic image approximates to the microcosm—become conventional. And if we should choose to argue, as I have here, that the indicative of conventional reference, as "ultimate subjunctive," is itself a certain strain of metaphor or trope, then the problem of condensed meanings involves the conventional also.

15. Sigmund Freud, *The Interpretation of Dreams* (London: The Hogarth Press, 1953).

The problem of "reading" elicited analogic flow can be countered to some extent by contextualization, using the pattern or tendency of other associated tropes as guides in the interpolative interpretation of a particular example. (Convention is perhaps, in this respect, social contextualization.) If we approach a set of cultural analogies, a ritual, for instance, as a contextual set in this way, then the understanding and explication of its individual metaphors may be illuminated by the strain or tendency of the whole; a general sense of the whole will inform the interpretation of its parts, and vice versa.

But if we can construct the ritual as a whole as a trope, then the contextual interrelationships among its components—its constituent tropes—will be relations of parts of a trope to the whole, and we will have parsed the trope. The force of the generic lies not in some "family resemblance" among the constituent images of a ritual, but in the holography of part and whole—the closure of the constituents to form a trope or metaphor in a larger frame of cultural significance. The whole is, in fact, the condensation, via the order of the generic, of the constituents, and condensation becomes, in this way, the order of cultural construction.

Returning now to my point of departure, the contrast between name as reference and name as analogic relation, it is clear that the dialectic of macrocosm and microcosm, as an analytic strategy, amounts to an encompassing of the entire symbolic continuum within the realm of analogic relations. Having discarded the Saussurian notion of "sign" as the frontier of abstraction (and, therefore, of symbolism), symbolic points of reference must themselves be treated as analogic constructs—metaphors—although they are in fact the limiting condition of metaphor. This means that the dialectic opposes the collective images of convention (including lexical codings) to the relatively macrocosmic images of whole perception in an interplay of restriction and expansion.

I have shown that name (or, of course, symbol) as "point of reference" has the effect of stopping or controlling the flow of analogy for social purposes. (A previously unnamed Daribi child may be named either *poai,* "named," or *poẓiawai,* "unnamed," analogically opposite aspects of the same sequence; but for purposes of naming and identification the play of analogy must stop *somewhere*, and so one is chosen.) Symbol as *image*, as the elicitation of multiple, condensed analogy, bridges between names as points of reference, bringing them into a relational field. The transition involved in expanding a metaphor into larger frames of cultural reference is a transformational expansion through a relational field, but it is also controlled by the exigencies of what I have called the "generic," the holography of trope expansion that is the formal concomitant of condensation.

If images and points of reference, macrocosm and microcosm, are indeed mediators, then they must achieve their signification—and their very constitution—in the act of mediation. A point of reference is significant, and significative, insofar as it mediates among points of reference. Thus the movement, or process of expanding point metaphors into frame metaphors, which I have called *obviation*,[16] embodies a movement back and forth across the dialectic until the mediation is resolved. Obviation may be seen as the dialectical resolution of mediation, the exhaustion of a mediator, and of the relations set up through it, as the mediation condenses into one of its poles. The obviation of image, at the macrocosmic pole, resolves itself in the formation of a conventional (or moral) metaphor relating the factual and the collective (fig. 3a); the obviation of convention, at the microcosmic pole, resolves itself in the formation of an individuative metaphor relating the factual and the collective (fig. 3b). In each case, mediative interaction within the dialectic (collapsed, in Fig. 3, into a linear movement, but best depicted as ternary opposition) leads to the encompassing of one pole by the other.

The expression that is formed by such a resolution takes over the whole function of the dialectic in mediating between social collective and factual embodiment. But this does not mean that it includes those aspects of actuality within its formal

16. Roy Wagner, *Lethal Speech: Daribi Myth as Symbolic Obviation* (Ithaca: Cornell University Press, 1978), chapter 1.

articulation: it cannot, for they are not symbolic—we know them only through the mediation of cultural reference and cultural image. The following chapter presents an ethnographic example of such a mediated dialectic, an obviation sequence. The recursiveness of the dialectic itself, and the external poles of social collectivity and embodied fact that it mediates, are constituted by exponential orders, or powers, of trope. I shall

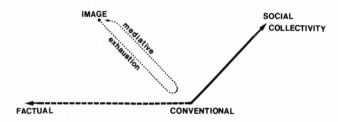

A: FORMATION OF A CONVENTIONAL TROPE

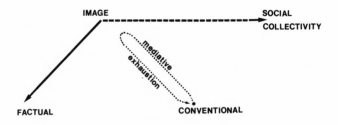

B: FORMATION OF AN INDIVIDUATIVE (FACTUAL) TROPE

FIGURE 3: Obviation as mediative resolution.

conclude this discussion of the dialectic by introducing the first and most immediately relevant of these, second-order trope.

The reversibility inherent in obviation—that the expansion from point to frame can move from microcosm to macrocosm *or* from macrocosm to microcosm—amounts to its enabling condition, the character of dialectic itself. This can be understood in terms of the notion of "back metaphor," noted above: that when the "as if" implied by a metaphor is established (as an "is"), the "is" of the conventional references becomes itself a metaphorical "as if." This reversibility amounts to superordinate principle, the second-order trope of figure-ground reversal, by which a perception can be inverted with its perceptual "ground." Hence the dialectic is enabled by its reversibility, by the fact that—albeit differentially and in different ways—referential microcosm and embodied macrocosm can serve alternately as figure and ground to one another.

Just as trope in our ordinary understanding amounts to a perception within a field of conventional reference, so figure-ground reversal is the *trope of perception*. It applies the principle of trope to trope itself, changing its orientation, and thus both enabling and bounding the scope of obviation.

3   Metaphor Spread Out:
The Holography of Meaning

The traditional approach to kinship studies, established by Louis Henry Morgan,[1] has been to assume that cultures fit themselves into a regime of "natural kinship," given by the "facts" of genealogy, by organizing a set of social roles that develop it into a system of institutions, rights, and marriage practices. Whether the "givenness" of natural kinship is assumed as an article of faith or as a useful "heuristic," it furnishes an unexamined and prepackaged ground of differentiation for an anthropology that would like to limit its scope to the study of collectivities and their organization.

An analogic approach, by contrast, begins with the centrality of relationship—the fact that all modes of "relating" are basically analogous—and asks how the differentiation of kinds of relationships, imposed by culture, controls the flow of analogy among them. It may be culturally appropriate, for instance, for an uncle to act "fatherly," or for a cousin to "be" a brother; but treating son or brother as lover or husband, or a mother or sister as paramour belongs often to the inappropriate flow of analogy that we call incest. Analogic kinship is a matter of maintaining a morally appropriate flow by balancing similarity against differentiation, keeping generation from turning into degeneration, as it were.

The *flow* of analogy, the interrelation among known, conventional relationships, articulates their sequentiality and significance in terms of cultural conceptions of generation, nurturance, or whatever other terms the myth of life might assume. The flow itself may be dealt with, in part, through the modes

1. The most extended and comprehensive discussion of this issue is David M. Schneider's *A Critique of the Study of Kinship*, (Ann Arbor: The University of Michigan Press, 1984).

34

and protocols in which people relate to one another—taboos, avoidances, joking, reciprocity—but its major symbols are usually those of body substance, spirit, or lineality. Understood as a native model of analogic flow, these symbols have less the character of "beliefs" or supports of a "structure" than that of motifs in a myth.

The Daribi myth or trope of life and generation, which I shall examine in this chapter, realizes its totality as part of a larger set of interlinked tropes, not as a model of marriage or society. Whatever other significances they may be seen to have, for social, economic, or ecological, purposes, Daribi kin relationships derive their indigenous meaning from the expansion of this trope.

We are dealing, then, with relationship in depth rather than with relatives; more than this, however, we are dealing with the relations among relationships, the regularities through which they are constituted, transformed, and resolved. The objective reality of such a regime of kin construction lies not in its referents—concrete behaviors, sets of people, or actual gene flows—but in the meanings, the perceptions, that it embodies in the course of its expansion into a large-frame metaphor. Let us now examine this expansion as it occurs among the Daribi people of Papua New Guinea.

Daribi kinship begins with the act of betrothal, with a restrictive interdiction of all social recognition (all direct "relating") between a man (and, usually, his male siblings) on one side, and his betrothed and her mother, on the other. They may not speak to each other, see each other, utter one another's name or the name of the thing it refers to, or hear such a name spoken. The principal parties, the man and his betrothed's mother, are ("true") *au* to each other; all interaction between them must be mediated and commuted to exchanges of wealth. An infringment of the interdict must be rectified by a small gift of wealth to the female *au;* the betrothal itself is formalized by the presentation of a sizable amount of "male" goods to the woman's line, and the return of a smaller payment.

The interdict is a *substitution* of affinal protocols, in the strongest sense, those of complete avoidance, for whatever other relational analogies (such as their being friends, or distant second cousins) that may have previously involved the persons concerned. This substitution, and the exchange through which it is effected, establishes a conventional restriction of social interaction, recognition, and presentation, a marked behavioral microcosm, among the principals to the betrothal and their close kin. I shall speak of it as substitution *A*. In addition to the *au* relationship, affinity involves that among *wąi*, a man (and his brothers) and the father (and father's siblings) of his betrothed, a guarded relationship in which the receivers of the betrothal show especial restraint and deference, and the similar but less strongly emphasized *bąʒe* relationship, between a man (and his brothers) and the siblings of his betrothed. The major sanction on this microcosm of relating through avoidance and respect is the social compromise known as *hare* ("embarrassment," or perhaps "shame": defined as "that which we feel in the presence of *wąi*"), so much so that the interdict might also be described as simply the imposition of *hare*.

Daribi marriages are traditionally initiated by betrothal or subsequently transferred betrothal (49.6% in a sample of 702 marriages[2]), or by leviratic transfer of wives (46.8%), and girls were often betrothed in infancy. Betrothals are said to be bestowed "in return for wealth and meat," and the expectation is that a relatively constant supply of meat will flow from the receiver of the betrothal to the girl's relatives. An imagery of meat and wealth pervades the whole affair: those who give generously can expect additional wives from the line of their *wąi* (16.7% of all contracted marriages after the first), and at some point in the affair the betrothed should visit the household of her future husband (chaperoned closely by his mother) "to see whether he is accumulating the bridewealth." Betrothal, then, amounts to the setting up of an analogy of relationship through a flow of detached, partible wealth items, traditionally meat and pearlshells. This "relationship" of "horizontally"

2. The statistics presented here were originally published in Roy Wagner, "Mathematical Prediction of Polygyny Rates among the Daribi of Karimui Patrol Post, Territory of Papua and New Guinea," *Oceania* 42, no. 3 (March 1972). Some supplementary statistics were published later in Roy Wagner, "Analogic Kinship: A Daribi Example," *American Ethnologist* no. 4 (1977).

flowing wealth is substituted for the expectation of ordinary human interaction that has been restricted by the interdict, and for any "flow" of common substance that could be seen to relate the parties beforehand. We can distinguish this analogical consequence of the interdict from the "vertical" flow of body substance that is felt to "relate" people. I shall speak of this as substitution B; it contrasts with the "conventional" substitution A in that it does not directly set up a social distinction, but rather models relationship analogically.

Daribi commonly speak of the betrothal of a woman as the "taking of her soul" *(noma'sabo)* by the prospective husband's line. A soul *(noma'* also means "shadow" or "reflection") is a partible identity, as the giving of meat and wealth is partible analogy, and the usage here is comparable to Mauss's notion of the Maori *hau,* as the spirit of a gift that compels reciprocation.[3] The *wegi noma'* ("girl-soul"), then, is the social identity of the betrothed "taken" as a kind of pledge for her ultimate bestowal as a return on the prestations of meat and wealth, the acknowledgment and affirmation of relationship as horizontal flow.

The act of marriage, *we kebo* (the "tying" or "fastening" of the woman, thus redeems the expectation or debt set up by the flow of prestations. In so doing it also grants the horizontal flow a distinct gender polarity, it "sexualizes" it by establishing a two-way flow of women (as female relatives of the bride now become normatively marriageable in the same direction) as against meat and wealth. This substitution, the conventional rite of marriage exchange that I shall identify as substitution C, condenses a rich spectrum of implications and perceptual possibilities into a single dramatic act.

The rite consists of the presentation of the bride price before the bride's father's house, and its acceptance by the bride. The groom and four or five other men of his line assume an attire called the *ogwanoma'* (literally "boy-soul," but spoken as one word): a covering of charcoal over the entire visible body, a

3. Marcel Mauss, *The Gift,* trans. Ian Cunnison (Glencoe, Ill.: The Free Press, 1954). See also the extended discussion of the Maori *hau* in Marshall Sahlins, *Stone Age Economics* (Chicago: Aldine Press, 1972), chapter 4.

black, cassowary-plume headdress, and contrasting white shell decorations—the traditional male battle dress. The men assume a tense, rigid stance, in single file facing the house door, maintain complete silence, and each holds some of the pearl shells—traditionally the major component of the bride price—in the left hand, and a bow and sheaf of arrows in the right. The bride emerges from the house splendidly attired, and walks down the file, collecting the pearlshells from each man, and then takes them to her father. As each man is relieved of his shells, he takes one of the arrows into his left hand and snaps rigidly back to "attention."

The "boy-soul" is the literal counterpart of the girl's "soul" that is "taken" in betrothal; it is displayed on the very occasion when the girl's "soul," so to speak, is replaced by the girl herself, and the promise of a woman in return for a flow of wealth is fulfilled. But the *ogwanoma'* itself is *not* transmitted but merely displayed; it is the pearlshells that are transmitted, and when this occurs they are very ostentatiously replaced with an arrow. Unlike the girl-soul, the boy-soul is *retained,* and retained in a martial posture; moreover the formation assumed by the groom's party is that which serves the Daribi as a metaphor for succession in birth order and lineality (*e turibadu,* "and at his back is . . ."). The groom's party and the *ogwanoma'* dramatize the continence of male *vertical* flow as against the horizontal outflow of male wealth. The bearing and demeanor of the men, furthermore, suggest the contingency of this flow; it is something to be defended and safeguarded.

The composition of the bride price and its counter prestation both emphasizes this gender identification and exposes its relativity. The bride price consists of male wealth—pigs, pearlshells, and adjuncts of male productive activity, such as axes and bushknives; it is divided into two parts: *were oromawai* ("given without return for the woman")—the part that goes as compensation for the woman—and *we pona siare* ("woman purchase-finished")—the part compensated for by the return payment given with the woman. This "dowry," called *sogwarema mabo,* consists largely or wholly of female wealth, artifacts and/or adjuncts of women's production, such as bark cloaks, net bags, and trade cloth. It is most significant that the woman is compensated for with items of *male* wealth; she is not "replaced," for instance, as a female, with a prestation of women's things. This is because she is viewed by her natal line as a part of their own vertical *male* flow, and her loss to this flow must be compensated for by male wealth. "We," for the Daribi, are always male contingency. (A bride's indebtedness to her maternal line is terminated at her marriage by a payment taken out of her bride price.) It is only the husband's line that sees the wife-givers as a female flow, and they represent themselves to the wife-takers through the giving of female wealth as well as women.

Substitution *C* marks a return to the conventional or microcosmic pole of the dialectic, establishing *B* as the analogical mediator between two points of conventional reference (betrothal and marriage). But it also stands as a Hegelian synthesis, mediating between the interdict set up in *A* and the horizontal flow of wealth in *B* by establishing a marital relationship through a reciprocation of the flow. It makes the horizontal flow sexually complementary, like the interdict, and supplements the interdict with a relationship; but it also retroactively motivates the sexual complementarity of the original interdict (*A*), providing a flow-based rationale for the pairing of male and female *au* as initiators (fig. 4).

As a point of mediation, *C* also (as indicated by the triangular configuration of fig. 4) stands *between* the microcosmic and macrocosmic poles represented by *A* and *B*; its status as a conventional point of reference is achieved by virtue of the analogy of horizontal flow provided by substitution *B*. Its constitution of a conventional metaphor through the construction of a female analogic counterflow is to that degree rendered somewhat arbitrary and relative, for it is "female" only in relation to the wife-takers. For the wife-givers, since every line perceives its own flow as male and vertical, it is a depletion, to be compensated with male wealth. Thus the construction renders itself transparent to the extent that it makes it obvious that the gender identity of the flow depends upon one's point of view.

This is the second meaning of "obviation" (making it a

metaphor of metaphoric effect); it renders its constructions progressively more *obvious* as their cumulative mediations of the dialectic become increasingly relative. As perceptual symbolizations mediating within their own constitutive flow, the stages of obviation become perceptions within that flow.

The first closure in the sequence of Daribi kin relations establishes analogic flow as the medium of kin construction. But the point of closure, at *C*, also serves as a point of reference mediating between two macrocosmic expressions, and therefore leads to a new "opening," via a Hegelian "antithesis," at substitution *D*. This substitution involves the procreative ac-

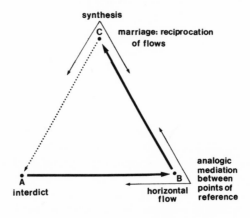

FIGURE 4: First closure in the Daribi kinship sequence.

tivity culminating in the birth of offspring, and is best understood via the Daribi notion of conception. Daribi consider maleness to be an effect of seminal fluid, *kawa,* contained and developed within a system of tubes *(agwa bono)* and nodes *(agwa ge)* that we know as the lymphatic system, and transmitted by a man in coitus. It flows around the blood in the uterus, and forms the outer layer of the embryo: the skin, eyes, teeth, and hair, as well as the lymphatic system and genitalia of a man, and the lymphatic system and mammary glands of a woman. Femaleness is considered to be an effect of maternal blood, *pagekamine,* contained within the circulatory system, and provided by the woman in the conception of a child. It forms the inner layer of the embryo: bones, viscera and other internal organs, and the circulatory system. Menstruation releases *pagekamine* for procreative purposes.

The crucial difference between these fluids and the characterisitcs they objectify is the relative contingency of maleness and of a man's supply of *kawa,* and the relative sufficiency of femaleness and of a womn's supply of *pagekamine.* Quantities of both fluids are necessary to the formation of an embryo, and although the amount of blood in a woman's body is always felt to be sufficient for this, the amount of seminal fluid that a man receives from his father is never sufficient for conception, and must be augmented. It is replenished and supplemented by the juices and fat of meat that is eaten, which enter the *agwa* system (in a woman they are transformed into maternal milk). Meat is, therefore, the external complement of male reproductive potential, its partible and portable accessory, and it is also, therefore, the link between horizontal and vertical analogic flow. The exigencies of acquiring, controlling, and assembling meat in the right quantities at the right times, since these activities are social and reciprocal ones, make male physical contingency into a social contingency. The Daribi put it succinctly: "we marry those (lines) with whom we do not eat meat."

The conception and birth of offspring, however, model what has heretofore been negotiated in terms of external analogy, the flow of gifts of meat and wealth as against the gifts of women and female goods, in terms of internal flow—that of bodily substance. The marriage that was enacted solely through the reciprocation of horizontal flows is now replicated analogically in the form of *vertical* flow, the substantial connection of parent to offspring, and of lineage to lineage. Thus the substitution of internal, vertical flow for external, horizontal flow (and of a "marriage" of fluids in the former for marriage in the latter) directly controverts and "cancels" the sense of interdict at *A,* which was to abrogate any relationship between the lines involved. We can, therefore, diagram this substitution, *D,* directly above *A,* because although it represents the opposite dialectical mode, it addresses the same issue as *A* (fig. 5).

Substitution *D* corresponds to the median point of the sequence, the state at which relationship, interdicted at the outset, comes into its own and begins to carry the external analogy of exchange along with it. This substitution also compounds the perceived relativization noted in substitution *C,* for the relativity of male as against female flow in that instance here becomes incarnate in the constitution of the cultural persona. The analogy that links person to person, and unit to unit (and it must be kept in mind that *every* person represents such an analogy),

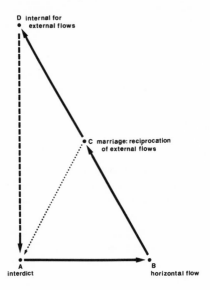

FIGURE 5: Cancellation of the interdict.

is perceived as male by the wife-givers (who regard their "sisters' children" attitudinally and terminologically as their *own*) and female by the wife-takers.

From its own point of view, each side regards the child that forms the analogy as its own internal flow, though conventional usage treats the resulting analogy from the viewpoint of the wife-takers, as a flow of *pagekamine,* or maternal blood. The child's maternal line, represented generally by a maternal uncle, are its *pagebidi,* "owners" or "base-people." Whichever point of view one adopts, however, the analogy serves to relate the two linealities involved and to erode and render ambiguous any expression of their distinctness.

Thus an additional conventional restriction, or social point of reference, is necessary to interdict the untempered flow of relational analogy. This takes the form of a modeling of external, or horizontal, flow upon internal (vertical) flow as the general social structural convention that I have called "normative patriliny."[4] It correlates the *sharing* of meat and wealth with male substantial flow, and the *exchanging* of meat and wealth with female *(pagekamine)* flow. As the definitive social statement of gender in relation to social constitution, it opposes male contingency—the necessity of men to pool and share meat and wealth for both social and physical procreation—to female sufficiency. The latter is manifested in the notion that the *pagebidi* have, by virtue of the bond of "base-blood," a kind of primordial right to the child that can be exercised by taking possession of the child in case of default by the father or, failing that, by cursing the child with illness or death.

Substitution *E,* internally motivated for externally motivated exchange, carries a wide range of social and perceptual implications. As a conventional expression it forms a synthetic closure to the thesis-antithesis sequence that begins with marriage at *C;* it organizes the two flows, brought together at *C,* and internalized at *D,* in terms of moral contingencies and priorities. As the definition point for male contingency and female sufficiency, it provides a retroactive motivation for the *ogwanoma* dramatization at the marriage rite. (*C*). As a modeling of horizontal flow or exchange directly upon internal, substantial flow, it controverts and cancels substitution *B,* the setting up of a horizontal flow *in lieu of* internal or vertical flow (fig. 6). Most significantly, it organizes the *pagehabo* payments that define lineality as against relational analogy, and the leviratic flow of wives *within* the lineality. Finally, as it fosters a flow of wives within the sharing unit, and a kind of sharing with the maternal uncle outside of the unit, substitution E advances the relativization of internal as against external flow almost to the limit.

Pagehabo (from *pagehaie,* "to pay the *pagebidi*") amounts to a series of substitutions of male wealth that is due to a child's *pagebidi* so as to redeem the child's health and membership status with regard to the *pagebidi's* prerogatives. *Pagehabo* is given a few years after birth, at initiation for males or marriage for females, and again at death. Payment is often delayed or negotiated, and is customarily demanded only for a woman's

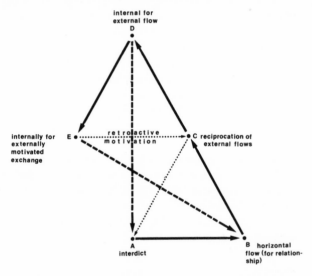

FIGURE 6: Second closure; cancelling of substitution B.

first three children. An adult man should pair off with one of his maternal uncles in an ongoing exchange relationship; the status of *pagebidi* with regard to a grown woman is commuted to her brothers at marriage (part of the retroactive motivation of substitution C by E, in which *wegi noma'* and *ogwanoma'* are cast in terms of female sufficiency and male contingency).

Pagehabo is relativized by the fact that, insofar as the child can be seen to share the lineality (especially that of male analogic flow) of the *pagebidi,* the payments can be construed as a *sharing* between child and *pagebidi.* This is particularly the case as a young man approaches adulthood, and begins to assume responsibility for making his own payments, and is emphasized in a popular custom. Most Daribi exchanges involve the reciprocation of a smaller prestation, called *sogwarema*, by the receivers of the main prestation. In the case of a male child, however, the *sogwarema* wealth will often be withheld by the *pagebidi* until the boy grows up and begins to assemble his bride price, and then be turned over to him for this purpose. Even if the *sogwarema* has not been withheld, however, a request to the *pagebidi* for a bride price contribution should be honored. However it is made, this contribution has the effect of turning "exchanging" into "sharing" among lineage mates, particularly since bride-price contributions are a significant indicator of such sharing.

Pagehabo models the exchange of wealth between units upon internal flow (to the point of modeling the relativization of this flow according to lineal viewpoint); the junior levirate models the exchange of wives upon internal analogic flow *within* the unit. Moreover, the normative model upon which the levirate is organized emphasizes flow: wife (or betrothal) inheritance should proceed lineally from elder to younger. The eldest of a set of male siblings is referred to as the *gominaibidi,* the "head man" or "source man," on the analogy of a *wę-gomo,* or "water head," the height at the source of a stream. (A "flow" from father to offspring is also encouraged, provided the woman did not nurture the latter.) The flow does not always correspond to this norm (though statistics indicate that it does in a majority of cases[5],) and there is a very small (3.8%) incidence of inheritance between maternal uncle and nephew.

"Sharing" in Daribi exchange generally connotes the sharing (giving, that is, without expectation of immediate return) of male wealth items; "exchanging" generally involves the giving of such wealth against a perceived female flow. By the time the child conceived in substitution D has reached adulthood, one has, even excluding such anomalies as leviratic exchange

5. Roy Wagner, "Analogic Kinship," 637. In a sample of 397 leviratic transfers, 216, or 54.3%, involved inheritance from a normatively preferred source of wives, 40, or 10.4%, from a permissible but not preferred source, the others being too distant to trace or ambiguous with regard to normative status.

between maternal uncle and nephew, a situation of sharing across lineal boundaries, and a flow of wives within male lineality. Relativization has reached the point where the normative alignment of sharing and exchanging with flow has been compromised, because the two kinds of flow have come to model one another completely. Thus the perception of arbitrariness in the distinction between the kinds of flow, first encountered in substitution *C*, has increased in acuity to the extent that a definite analogy can be discerned between them. This analogy, then, mediates the final transition.

The children, respectively, of a brother and sister are related through a combination of male and female ties (taking into consideration the perspective of the sister's husband's line); the man who is *pagebidi* to one set is father to the other. These cross-cousins, or *hai'*, as Daribi call them, belong generally to distinct and separate patrilines, lines that remain distinct by virtue of the *pagehabo* given to mediate the ("female") analogic link between them. But it is also true that the same man who shares bride wealth with one set of males as their father shares it with the other set as *pagebidi*, that, because of mutual modeling, the two flows that meet in this man become the same flow. Daribi say that *hai'* "are the same as siblings," that they should treat one another and think of one another as siblings. Indeed, insofar as male and female analogic flow can be seen as equivalent, as the "same" flow, *hai'* are like siblings. Insofar as a discrimination can be made between the kinds of flow, the metaphor of "siblingship" becomes qualified. This qualification involves the fact that male matrilateral *hai'* are characterized as *pagebidi*, and may be referred to as *dwano pagebidi* ("little *pagebidi*"); they are entitled to share the wealth from ego's *pagehabo* payments, and may exercise the *pagebidi's* curse.

The normative relationship among *hai'* is, despite the qualification, grounded in the equivalence of the two kinds of flow and the "siblingship" implied thereby. Thus male *hai'* should contribute to one another's bride prices, as brothers should, and they are entitled to a share in the bride wealth received for their respective female *hai'*, as with sisters. As "brothers," male *hai'* may exercise a claim (rated as being just below that of a younger brother in priority) on the inheritance of one another's

widows. But because of the qualification, and specifically, perhaps, because the equivalence of the flows is mediated by a
mutual "sharing" of wealth with the *pagebidi* of the qualifying
link, the rights and obligations of *hai'* are expressed through
the idiom of exchanging. The leviratic claims of *hai'* must,
therefore, be validated by equilateral exchanges among the respective co-heirs (payments that are refundable should the inheritance not take place). Beyond this, the matrilateral asym-
metry is coded as a slight implication of leviratic seniority on
the part of a patrilateral *hai',* who, if a *gominaibidi* (the eldest
male of his sibling series), should not inherit the widow of his
hai'pagebidi, "because his mother came from there." In a sense,
the flow of *pagehabo* wealth to the matrilateral *hai'* is transformed, via the siblingship metaphor, into a quasi-lineal flow
of wives.

Substitution F emerges as an analogic consequence that
"happens to" the conventional restriction of substitution E as
the two kinds of flow come to model one another. We can
speak of the substitution of equivalence of flows for normatively distinct male and female flows, an expression that serves
to controvert and cancel the "marriage" of distinct and opposed
flows in substitution $C,$ and that stands in a relation of obviative
implication to the interdict, $A,$ that initiated the sequence (fig.
7). If relationship is commuted to analogic flow, and the flow
is sexually reduplicated, and the reduplication is internalized,
the internalization modeling external exchange, which in turn
melds the two internal flows into one, then we arrive at a
universal, nongendered relational analogy, derived ultimately
from the interdict, but absolutely antithetical to its (gendered,
abrogation of relationship) intent. This can be expressed, in
the terms of this analysis, as a final substitution, $G,$ coterminous
with $A,$ the original imposition of the interdict, but supplanting
it.

Such a substitution, being so strongly implied, is in no more
need of execution than a mating move in chess. But it would
be useful indeed, for analytical purposes, to determine the nature of the substitution and its range of implication. As the
obviational supplanter of substitution $A,$ it stands in a negative
or antithetical relation to it; but it is also, because of its position

in the diagram (i.e., coterminous with *A*), placed in a relation of mutual controversion and cancellation with substitution *D*. As the negation, or "not," of *A*, it is also in the rather paradoxical situation of being the "not" of *D*, itself the "not" of *A*: it is in fact what Richard Schechner would call the "not-not" of *A*—the negation of its negation that is yet not the thing itself. It has been noted above that the obviating antithesis of *A*, arrived at via the melding of internal flows through external wealth exchange, would be some form of universal, nongen-

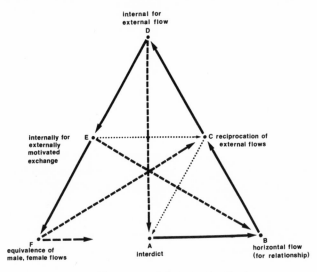

FIGURE 7: The point of obviative implication.

dered relational analogy. Considering the role of external flow in mediating *F*, as well as the terms of substitution *D* (internal, vertical flow, via conception, for external flow), it becomes apparent that this "not-not" involves also some kind of *external* conception, that is, one involving wealth objects.

We can write substitution *G*, then, as "universal relational analogy via conception through wealth objects for internal relationship through equivalence of flows," and understand this to mean that human beings are all interrelated through the circulation of meat and pearlshells, which, though ungendered, "reproduce" human beings by moving externally and inversely to their own analogic flow.

Substitution *G* forms the synthetic closure of the third dialectical mediation in the sequence, and also realizes the resolution of the sequence itself. As a synthesis, *G* mediates between the internal modeling of external flow or exchange at *E*, and the equation of internal flows, mediated by exchange, at *F*, in its assertion of the paralleling of universal internal flow by a universal external flow. The flow of meat and pearlshells

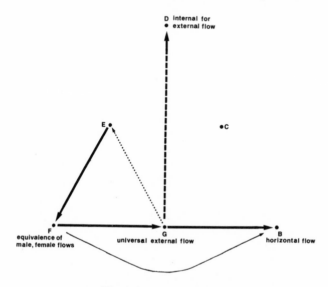

FIGURE 8: Third closure; resolution of the sequence.

elicits universal substance analogy. This supplies a retroactive motivation to the "sharing" between an adult man and his *pagebidi* in substitution *E*, for the flow of wealth elicits an "internal" analogic relationship between them (fig. 8).

As the "not-not" of substitution *A*, *G* marks the ultimate stage in relativization, for it poses the paradox of universal relationship via the external, partible wealth objects that were substituted for relationship in *B*. In another sense, however, the sequence never ends, for *G* (supplanting *A*) forms the mediative transition between the equivalence of internal flows via external flow, in *F*, and external flow in lieu of relationship, in *B* (fig. 8).

Substitution *G* is clearly not the "result" or summation of the sequence as a whole, but rather a kind of ultimate limit, where relativization has resonated through to an exhaustion of its possibilities. Ambiguous in that it both referentially negates and negatively references *A*, *G* is also ambivalent in that it both marks the conclusion of the sequence, by supplanting its beginning point, and also facilitates its continuance by bridging between *F* and *B*. The consequence of the sequence is the formation of a large-frame metaphor of bilateral relationship through the obviation and exhaustion of restrictive kin convention or point of reference (as in fig. 3B). The *meaning* of the sequence, because it encompasses the development of a "symbol that stands for itself," is embodied in its working out, and also exhausted in the process.

Because it requires several generations for its working out, but largely because its transition points form the stable axes of long-term relationships among people, and because any given person may engage a number of different axes simultaneously, the sequence is seldom apparent as such. The tendency, for Daribi as well as for outsiders, is to focus on the relatively fixed combinations and complementarities among relationships-families, lineages, kin terminologies, and the like. But if we keep in mind that the thing modeled here as "flow," in its various forms and transitions, is neither meat, nor pearlshells, nor blood, nor semen, but relational meaning, then it is clear that the openings and closings of the obviation sequence are the pulse that drives families, lineages, and kin terminologies. Kin organization is the way in which people perceive and enact their relationships with one another, and obviational flow models that perception and enactment. A trope that negotiates the transformation of microcosmic kin restrictions and conventions into macrocosmic relationship, the sequence we have followed is also the processual enactment of a myth, the myth of Daribi kinship.

Obviation as process encompasses the very same operation as does the formation of a trope out of symbolic points of reference. We can, therefore, speak of any instance of trope, or tropelike usage, as an instance of obviation, and consider an obviation sequence, such as the one we have just explored, as a trope. Any verbal explication of the process or diagrammatic analysis is adequate and helpful only insofar as it remains faithful to the holographic correspondence between point metaphor and frame metaphor. Because a true holographic correspondence involves a degree of condensation, or image intensity, and recursiveness that defies reduction to the linear and referential relations necessary for analysis, however, my explication of the obviational process cannot adequately describe or enact the process itself, but only serve to *elicit* it, as a verbal metaphor elicits a trope. A trope cannot "happen" in words or diagrams, but only as a result of the analogic or interpretive "competence" of those who perceive them, and therefore perceive *through* them. It is completely *ad hominem,* and *ex hominem.*

What appears as a dialectic, even an involute, recursive dialectic, is actually a dialectic at work mediating its own polarity, moving into, and through, its own *limen,* and, if we are lucky, facilitating a perception of its own constitution in the process. A verbal explication is adequate insofar as it can elicit verbal tropes (metaphors of metaphor) to "figure" the process; a "structural" diagram is adequate insofar as its structure is obviated to the same end. Taken together, the verbal and structural explications can serve to elicit the tropic movement that neither of them can adequately convey by itself.

Thus the diagrammatic explication that I have introduced as a "generic" of large-frame metaphors is totally artificial and introduced, a "model." It is not obviation, but a condensation of the Hegelian dialectic and the ternary diagramming of mediation into a closed, recursive format. Its main virtue is that it packs a number of complex interrelationships into a concise image—a counterpart at the macrocosmic pole of the microcosmic sequence of verbal explication. As words elicit trope, so image models the holographic expansion of point-referential trope into a larger whole.

Holography means that the substitutions we have encountered in analyzing Daribi kin relations realize their whole meaning ("meaning" considered as a perception in referential value space) solely through their integration within the larger trope. Any other consideration of them, for instance, as aspects of a social structure, is subsidiary to this point. Holography also implies that linear correlates of condensation can be retrieved by "unpacking" the diagrammatic model into its constituent mediations, and that this can be done in a number of ways. The *imagery* of the expansion from point metaphor to frame metaphor is that of the ternary, mediative-dialectical format that we encountered in examining the dialectic of perception and reference, and the holographic condensation of this imagery involves the universal replication of the overall format within all of its constituent relations.

Among the possible "deconstructions" of the model are a number that can help provide conjunctive elicitations of the movement and resolution of Daribi kin obviation. One of these—that of three successive mediations and mediative closures, dovetailed such that the concluding substitution of each corresponds to the beginning of the next—we have been following in the preceding pages and diagrams as our guide to the obviation process. The first closure completes the articulation of kin relations, via betrothal and marriage, in terms of external, analogic flow; the second resolves the internalization of flow into a normative system; the third realizes the analogy of a universal, bilateral relationship, but does so in terms of external, analogic flow, and so rejoins the sequence, via a paradoxical substitution, at its beginning point.

In the triangular metaphor of mediation, a point of synthesis must stand between the thesis and antithesis that it mediates. But in an ongoing dialectic, the *next* point, the antithesis to the synthesis, is itself the synthesis of a series of three beginning with the previous antithesis, and excluding the original thesis. The recursiveness of the obviation diagram registers this exclusion as a cancellation, in that every fourth point is situated opposite the first point on the figure, and represents the opposite "side" or pole of the dialectic (fig. 9A). Thus substitution *D* controverts and cancels *A, E* cancels *B,* and *F* cancels *C.* Each cancellation represents a step in the total obviation, until the paradoxical point *G* is reached, at which point a double cancellation (or a cancellation of cancellation—the equivalent of obviation) occurs.

If we follow the consecutive cancellations, *D–A, E–B,* and *F–C,* it becomes apparent that the mediative series *D–E–F* has

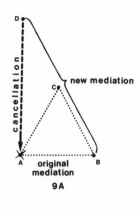

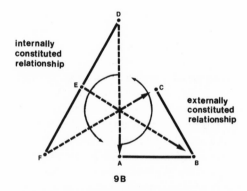

FIGURE 9: Cancellation and axial encompassment.

replaced the series *A–B–C,* or in other words that the constitution of relationship through conception and internal (vertical) analogy has encompassed the constitution of relationship through external (horizontal) analogy (fig. 9B). The movement of obviation here takes the form of a counterclockwise twist of the axis of cancellation, until it reaches the paradox of self-encompassment (*G–D*).

Each image of movement presented thus far has been dialectical; forward movement has proceeded from pole to pole of the dialectic until a point of dialectical contradiction is reached: the original point becomes part of a paradox, the axis of cancellation cancels itself. Concurrently, a sequence of encompassment takes place: each successive closure can be said to encompass its predecessor, in that it includes the previous synthesis in its mediation, and resolves that mediation with a new synthesis; the movement of cancellation proceeds to nullify the original mediation, point by point, until it is supplanted by the final one. Each version of this sequence is, likewise, dialectical. But it is also possible to view the sequence atemporally, as the direct encompassment of one dialectical pole or mode by the other.

The overall shape of the diagram corresponds to a mediating triangle, *B–D–F*, comprising one of the poles or sides of the dialectic (fig. 10). In the case of Daribi kin relations, this agentive or obviating mode is the macrocosmic. Between each two points on this larger mediative scheme a point corresponding to the opposite pole or side is placed, in the order of dialectical alternation. These points belong to the *obviated* mode, in this case the microcosmic, and they are points of opening and closure. As each closure is reached, a retroactive implication or motivation (shown in fig. 10 as a dotted line) is extended back to the "thesis" or opening point to complete the mediation. Thus, in the completed figure, an inscribed mediative triangle is precipitated within the outline of the obviating triangle by the retroactive implications of each closure. This triangle, *A–C–E*, amounts to a mediation within the encompassed or obviated mode.

The dialectic is generated by the intermediation of a macrocosmic and a microcosmic mediative triangle. But, whereas motion in the encompassing mode moves forward and carries the movement of the sequence as a whole, that in the encompassed mode moves backward in time against it (note the direction of *A–C–E* in fig. 10), augmenting the relativity of its perceptions through the implications of future resolutions. Retroactive implication gives the actor a glimpse of the futility and arbitrariness of the undertaking, against which he may redouble his efforts and his commitment. It corresponds to what I have called the "precipitation" or "counterinvention"[6] of one mode in the course of deliberate construction or articulation

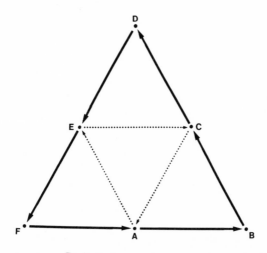

FIGURE 10: Dialectical encompassment and conterinvention.

within the other. As obviation progresses, the process itself becomes transparent and relativized to the point where this internal motivation overpowers the actor's will to resist it.

This aspect of the model suggests that human beings act against their perception of relativization. To what extent, then, does the expanding perception entailed in Daribi kin obviation culminate in a realization of the sequence as a whole, as impressionism depicted the painter's awareness of his own technique,

6. Roy Wagner, *The Invention of Culture* (Chicago: University of Chicago Press, 1981), 45–49.

or as twelve-tone music played upon the arbitrariness of the traditional scale? The perception at point G, of wealth moving in a cycle of "external conception" to generate an internal flow of relationship, can be understood as the transverse movement of wealth among clans against the flow of human marriage and procreation. Does such a transverse flow operate within the sequence of meanings as well? The inscribed triangle, A–C–E (or A–E–C) models a mediation among the three crucial conventional *exchanges* or prestations: betrothal, marriage, and child price, as the encompassing triangle B–D–F models the three analogic flows that mediate among these exchanges. Because Daribi (traditionally) betroth their daughters in infancy, at a time when the wealth received in betrothal payments is most in demand for *pagehabo* payments for the daughter and her siblings, it will most likely be used this way, and flow from A to E. We have seen, too, that a Daribi maternal uncle will withhold the *sogwarema* reciprocation for *pagehabo* payments until his nephew is assembling his bride price, so as to "share" with him and make a contribution. This wealth will flow from E to C, when the nephew uses it in marriage. Finally, Daribi usage explicitly marks the wealth received for a girl's bride price for her male siblings to use in betrothing wives of their own, so that *this* received wealth flows from C to A.

The reality of a transverse cycle of wealth—in this case wealth that can be kept and accumulated—pearlshells, moving *against* the obviation cycle can serve to answer a burning question that may be forming in the reader's mind: What, if not some kind of mystical prescience, is the *agency* of retroactive motivation and its entailed relativization? It is clear that this relativization is carried by the transverse, retrograde movement of pearlshells against the flow of analogy that figures kin relationship. Pearlshells in this sense embody the relativizing of the life process; they and the considerations and debts they entail restrict, channel, and redistribute the flow of relationship like a sort of escapement mechanism. Immortal themselves, they flow unendingly among clans and backwards against the relationships that constitute those clans.

The metaphor of Daribi kin relationship is a trope of analogic conception and flow formed against the retrograde flow of pearlshells. The flow of pearlshells forces life forward against its own relativization; life forces pearlshells backward in time, obviating their cycle and in the process obviating itself.

Thus the myth or genre of relationship, with its own internal oppositions, relations, contradictions, and relativization, unfolds as a self-motivating and ultimately self-assimilating invention, a symbol that stands for itself. It is also, however, a macrocosmic metaphor mediating symbolically between actuality and the social collectivity, and formed by the exhaustion of the cultural dialectic that spans them. But it represents only one possible mediation within this larger span, and to speak of it as self-contained serves only to pose the question of its relation to the other genres or myths of Daribi culture. What of pearlshells, and of the social shame or estrangement invoked in the affinal interdict that begins the sequence? The invention of this particular genre is contexted in a range, a dialectic, of other myths and genres. Let us explore this context by turning, in the chapter that follows, to some other examples.

4   Death on the Skin: Mortality and Figure-Ground Reversal

"The early bird gets the worm."
—American folk saying

"Everything has its worms."
—Daribi folk saying

When I first questioned some Daribi people about the mechanics of human reproduction, I was told that "we are not like birds, which eat a lot of fruit, and then produce eggs as excrement." This was a significant statement, because Daribi use the same word, *ge,* for the definitive traditional wealth item, the crescent pearl oyster *(Pinctada maxima)* ornament, as well as for birds' eggs. A potent metaphor is developed from the dual implications of this word: as the detached agent of "external conception" that cycles against the flow of human relationship, and as the "wealth object" that birds produce out of their own bodies and life processes, and which then hatches out into offspring. In effect, the "eggs" of human beings are immortal—they move externally and opposite to the flow of human reproduction, causing it without ever hatching, whereas birds produce their "pearlshells" out of their own bodies, only to see them destroyed in the production of offspring. People reproduce against the flow of their immortal *ge;* birds reproduce by moving *through* their mortal *ge.* This metaphor serves as the principal motivating element in a series of Daribi origin myths,[1] and it also serves to link between the genre of Daribi kin

1. Roy Wagner, *Lethal Speech: Daribi Myth as Symbolic Obviation* (Ithaca: Cornell University Press, 1978), chap. 2.

relationship and its grounding in the larger issues of morality and cosmogony.

Birds, introduced as an "antithesis," extend the reference point *ge* into a metaphor, and if obviation truly involves the expansion of point metaphors into larger cultural frames, then, knowing the generic, it should be possible to trace out the implications of this most potent one. *Ge* is used in unmodified form with reference to pearlshell, and may or may not be modified (*ba' ge,* "bird-*ge*") when referring to eggs; beyond this it enjoys a wide application as a classifier for objects of a relatively spherical conformation (an earlobe is an "ear-*ge*," an embryo a "child-*ge*," a puddle a "water-*ge*"), though the sun and moon ("sun-*ge*," "moon-*ge*") are explicitly said to be pearlshells. Thus the procreative metaphor encountered here does not by any means universalize or exhaust the linguistic possibilities of the word; it focuses a particular "band" of analogy, involving the word's most common referential usages in a tropic elicitation of the human condition.

Human beings are constituted through an immortal external and a mortal internal flow, birds are constituted through a single flow with alternate, mortal, internal and external phases; but in one important way Daribi consider human beings and birds to be similar. Both belong to the "lineage" of creatures whose skin is covered with *niʑi* ("hair, fur, or feathers"), the *niʑiʑibi.* As such they stand together in contrast to the *niʑimeniaiʑibi,* the "lineage without hair, fur, or feathers," reptiles, amphibians, eels, fish, worms, and insects. Like birds, the *niʑimeniaiʑibi* are seen as egglayers, but unlike birds and human beings, they are felt to be immortal. Exemplified particularly by the snake, these creatures do not die, in Daribi thinking, when they grow old, but merely shed their old skins and renew their lives.

Thus the snake occupies a medial and synthesizing position between human beings and birds. Like both, it reproduces with *ge,* and like birds, *ge* and organism are united in a single flow; unlike birds, however, the snake continues the hatching process beyond the egg—it sheds its skin and thus *hatches out of itself* into immortality. Like human beings, then, the snake forms a contrast with its *ge* in terms of mortality, but it is the opposite contrast, for in this case the creature is immortal and the *ge* are mortal.

When we turn from the relations among human beings via their pearlshells to the relation between human beings and their pearlshells, we pass, by means of a metaphor, into a paradigmatic comparison of the human condition with that of other living creatures. It should not be surprising to find, as we do, this analogic explication of the human relation to pearlshells as the first closure of the principal Daribi myth of human mortality. This is the story of Souw's Curse,[2] which Daribi tend to withhold as a kind of secret knowledge, though it is linked, via their neighbors on the lower Erave and Purari[3] rivers, with a widespread tradition of similar myths ranging to the southwest along the Papuan coast.[4] I have previously published translations of a number of textual variants from the Daribi and their neighbors; the following is a synoptic composite of the Daribi versions:

> Long ago, when human beings did not know
> death or the motives and implements of killing,
> two women were making sago flour. One had
> pendulous breasts, and the other had upright
> breasts. They heard a bird, called *kaueri* calling:
> when people hear this bird, they know it has

2. Translated texts are published in Roy Wagner, *The Curse of Souw: Principles of Daribi Clan Definition and Alliance* (Chicago: University of Chicago Press, 1967), 38–41, and idem, *Habu: The Innovation of Meaning in Daribi Religion* (Chicago: University of Chicago Press, 1972), 24–36.

3. A version of the Souw story featuring a hero named Soi was discovered by Brian J. Egloff and Resonga Kaiku among the Pawaiian speakers of the Purari River. This effectively links the interior distribution of the myth in the Karimui area with the much wider distribution along the Papuan coast. See Brian J. Egloff and Resonga Kaiku, *An Archaeological and Ethnographic Survey of the Purari River (Wabo) Dam Site and Reservoir* (Port Moresby: Office of Environment and Conservation and Department of Minerals and Energy, Papua New Guinea, 1978), appendix 6.

4. See Wagner, *Habu*, 19–24. There are recent indications that this complex of tales may be related to premodern activities of Ceramese bird-of-paradise traders on the Papuan south coast.

sighted a snake, and they go to the bush to hunt
it. As long as the woman with pendulous breasts
went to the bush, things went well—people did
not die, or steal, or work sorcery. But this time
the young girl, with upright breasts, went. She
saw a long, snakelike object rising from a ra-
vine—it was the penis of Souw. It tried to enter
her, but she cried out in fear and Souw, ashamed,
withdrew his penis. Then Souw made ready to
leave the place, and as he left he cursed mankind
with death, feuding, sorcery, and the other evils
that burden them. He threw down the weapons
used in fighting, the practices of stealing, adul-
tery, fighting, and sorcery, and the mourning
practices that follow upon death. People took up
these things and made use of them. Souw also
threw down his own skin, the shedding of which
renders one youthful. If people had recovered
this along with the evil practices, they would still
have been immortal, but instead the snakes and
hairless creatures took it, and now they alone do
not die. Souw traveled from this place, creating
the land and the ridges as he went, so that people
could not follow him. [In some versions his
daughter follows him, cutting passages through
the ridges with a stone knife.].

The myth begins with a primordial state in which human
beings, like pearlshells, are immortal; as with birds and snakes,
there was no separation of an internal as against an external
reproductive flow. The substitution that forms this primordial
and premortal state *(A)* involves the incorporation within human life processes of the immortal flow of *ge* as, in the Daribi
view, this occurs presently among snakes. The two flows were
one. Thus reproduction and nurturance were the same thing.
Sago flour, which the women are processing at the outset, is
the traditional and archetypal Daribi women's food product—
a vegetable food. It poses the question of the complementary

meat food, a male product (particularly since sago itself is a complementary crop—it is grown and felled by men, and processed by women); the answer is given by the bird's call, and by a retroactive implication from substitution *C*.

The bird, a *kaueri*, gives its characteristic cry announcing that it has sighted a snake. It is calling for a woman to come and kill the snake for meat, and thus furnishes a social pretext for one of the women to leave the other and go to the bush. But since reproduction and nurturance are the same thing, each is modeled on the other, and the women partake of their complementary meat-food by incorporating the meat-derived *agwa* flow in sexual intercourse. Thus "killing the snake" for meat refers to the bringing about of penile detumescence in the sexual act so as to incorporate the liquid essence of meat. The bird's invitation to this consummate repast is singularly appropriate, because as an egglayer it "marks" the nurturative-internal and sexual-external as distinct phases in its single flow, but as a mortal being laying mortal *ge,* it models each aspect of this flow on the other. Its "message," substitution *B,* is that the nurturative (and mortalizing) act of killing and eating meat and the procreative act of intercourse are analogues of each other.

A complementarized, experienced woman might be expected to "read" this message, but not a virgin. When the woman "with upright breasts" makes rendezvous with the "snake" in the bush, and it reveals itself as a penis attempting to enter her (substitution *C*: penis for snake), she cries out in fear, anticipating *her* literal death in place of the snake's figurative one (a relativization motivated by a retroactive implication from *E.*). The revelation of the snake as a penis at *C* provides a retroactive motivation for substitution *A,* human beings as immortal beings, for it shows the penis as the snakelike implement of a continually enacted rejuvenation, shedding its (fore)skin in the erectile act by which the flow of vital fluid is passed from man to woman.

The scream of the virgin, seeing her own death instead of the snake's, brings about an external and "social" detumescence in place of a copulative one, and a rejection of the primordial,

internal nutritive flow. Thus a social disjunction is imposed
between man and woman, the shame—the definitive social
emotion—whose physical equivalent is the loss of erection.
Substitution D, social detumescence (shame) for physical, abrogation of flow, has the effect of cancelling A, the internalization of immortal, external flow, for the flow has been interdicted between man and woman.

In retribution, now, for the shame, the untimely "death" of
his penis, Souw, the "snake," calls for the death of humankind
(reversing the sense and the polarity of the bird's call for the
"death" of the snake in B), cursing humanity with death, and
"throwing down" the motives, techniques, and observances of
killing and death. This motivates the relativization of C, in
which the virgin perceives the snake to be "killed" as her own
potential killer. Substitution E replaces the immortal internal
flow, abrogated in D, with a proffered external means of immortality via Souw's sheddable skin, itself a relativization produced by a retroactive implication from G. In its substitution
of humanity for the "snake" of B, and of the internal "eating
of meat" indicated by the bird for the disposable exterior of
Souw's skin, E controverts and cancels substitution B. (Both
are vocalizations.)

The proffered possibility of an immortality like the snake's,
in lieu of the broken internal flow of meat fluids, is not accepted.
Instead of humanity, the snakes and other hairless creatures
take up Souw's skin, and thus they replace human beings as
immortal creatures. Substitution F, snakes and other hairless
creatures for human beings (as immortal), thus inverts and
cancels C, human penis for (or as) snake. It also controverts A
in denying human immortality, and leads to the replacement
of A with G.

As the "not-not" of A, G must negate both the "internalization of immortal, external flow" of A, and also the abrogation
of flow in substitution D, and it must also resolve the final
mediation sequence E–F–G. It does so by replacing the snakes
and hairless creatures of F with ge, a kind of external "shell"
different from a sheddable skin, but an immortal one neverthe-
less. Reproduction through ge involves a flow, cancelling the

abrogation of flow in *D,* but the flow is external, as against the
internal flow of *A.* Finally, as *A* began the myth with a sociality
of two women, and *D,* at its midpoint, concerns an abrogation
between a man and a woman, so *G,* the not-not of obviation,
resolves into a flow of objects that may only pass from man to
man.

The retroactive flow of implication in this myth develops a
motivating relativization based on the perception of human
contingency as a condition of life or reproduction. Thus the

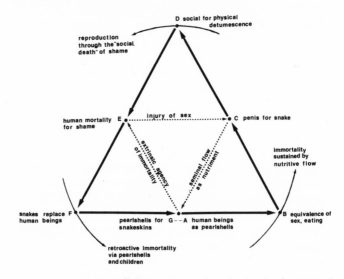

FIGURE 11: Relativization and motivation in the story of
Souw.

implication of *G,* perceived at *E,* of an extrinsic (e.g., nonin-
ternal) agency of human immortality, motivates the "throwing
down" of Souw's skin; this, in turn, "sets up" the snakes' supplanting of humanity by seizing the skin. And so mankind is
"immortal" retroactively only, through the backward flow of
pearlshells and the engendering of children (fig. 11). The
implication of *E,* perceived at *C,* is that of the injury of sex, the
contingency in which genital connection is achieved (penetration of a virgin, in this case), and it motivates the virgin's

rejection of Souw and his "social detumescence." Humanity thus reproduces through the social "death" of shame—connection achieved despite the implication of injury. Finally, the implication of C, perceived at A, is that the "meat" complement of nutriment in immortal life is administered in copulation, providing the "hunting" excuse of the mature, experienced woman and the trap that snared the virgin (and humanity) in the coils of mortality. The suggestion here is that the contingent flow of seminal fluid through the *agwa* system of males was once a completed nutritive flow between men and women that sustained their immortality without the necessity of reproduction.

If we approach this relativization from the proper perspective of the myth, as "resistance" to its forward movement, we encounter seminal flow first, as the primordial sustenance of immortality. Human beings were immortal; but copulation was necessary. Copulation was familiar for the experienced; but the virgin saw it as death. The virgin's reaction caused shame, and the curse that made a perceived demise into a human condition; but Souw also offered his skin. Snakes took the skin; so now humanity is immortal only through pearlshells (reproduction). The order of these substitutions suggests what we would experience if we began at D, the point of conception, in the Daribi kin relationships sequence, and proceeded toward E, and then onward: internal flow—shame—external flow.

If we invert the axes of cancellation in the diagram for Daribi kin relationships (fig. 7), transposing A and D, B and E, and C and F, we will produce a pattern of substitutions remarkably like that of the Souw myth (fig. 12). For A in the myth, the internalization within human life processes of the immortal flow of *ge*, is like the internalization of flow at conception (D in the kin sequence); B in the myth, the cry of the bird that models *ge* and organism on each other, is like the normative modeling of internal and external flows *(E)*; C, revealing the snake as a penis, resembles the equation of internal flows *(F)* in the equation of the two as "meat"; D, social detumescence and the origin of shame, is like the social interdiction of relationship between a man and his betrothed (and her mother—

A); *E,* the curse of death and Souw's offer of his skin as a final chance, is like the substitution of an external, horizontal flow for relationship *(B),* and *F,* snakes for human beings, is like the reciprocation or replacement of male flow by female in the act of marriage. The "not-not" point is similar in both sequences because in each it must negate the same two points, *A* and *D,* and these have merely been interchanged.

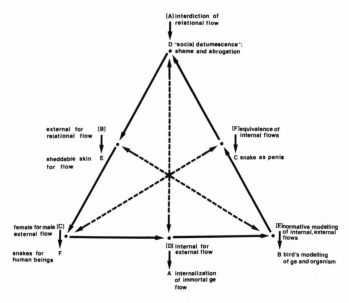

FIGURE 12: Souw myth sequence as axial inversion of kin sequence.

As obviations, the Daribi sequence of kin relations and the myth of Souw's curse are *axial inversions* of one another; that is, the "encompassing" *D–E–F* of each is the "encompassed" *A–B–C* of the other (fig. 13A), and the "encompassing" external triangle of each, *B–D–F,* becomes the "encompassed" inscribed triangle, *A–C–E,* of the other (fig. 13B). Since the latter triangles represent, respectively, the poles of the symbolic continuum (microcosmic and macrocosmic), the inversion is polar:

Daribi kin relationship emerges as a factual metaphor through the obviation of the conventional, and the Souw myth emerges as a moral account via the obviation of the factual—an unusual format for an origin myth, which is ordinarily concerned with

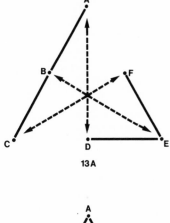

13A

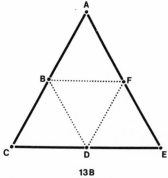

13B

FIGURE 13: Effective inversions between the Souw myth and the kin sequence.

the derivation of some factual condition or aspect of worldview. In this case, however, we are dealing with "conditions" that ground the morality of Daribi kin relations and social life: the contingency of male seminal flow and its modeling in exchange *(B)*, shame *(D)*, and mortality that makes humanity contingent on extrinsic means for reproduction *(F)*. These, then, are the microcosmic substitutions in the myth of Souw's curse, and they correspond to their axial opposites, *E, A,* and *C,* in the kin relationship sequence.

The points in the myth of Souw through which analogy expands, the sexual separation through social separation (shame) to the final separation of death, constitute, in the inversion of this expansion, a kind of escapement mechanism of exchanges that hold and channel the expansion of kin relationship. And the images through which kin relationship expands from gift exchange through the creation of human beings to the universal relationship of human beings become, in their inversion, the turning points of a myth of mortality. Each myth, that of life and that of mortality, is the reverse expansion of the other; what is "figure" and figuration to one is "ground," the obviated ground of resistance, to the other.

Because meaning, meaningful analogy, is a matter of perception, because it works through the view of the actor or witness, it effects obviation by the changes it makes in that view. When this flow of perceptual change becomes an instance of seeing vital antitheses as differential perspectives through the same basic points of orientation, then the difference between life and death becomes a matter of what gestalt psychology calls "figure-ground reversal."

Trope expands into cultural frame by obviating its initial conditions; the "not-not," or point of obviation *(G)*, marks the limit of the expansion of first-order trope where it emerges or resolves itself into the reversibility of second-order trope. If first-order trope is a perception within conventional reference points, then second-order trope, the "trope" of trope in the ordinary sense, is a dialectical shift in the orientation or perspective of the perceiver. Thus the second power of trope "holds" or "enables" the cultural dialectic, for when the flow of analogy reaches this power, it automatically reverts to the beginning point of the opposite expansion. Again, "perspective" and "orientation" ground a crucially important set of collective values and collectively elicited images here, rather than issues of analytic convenience or aesthetic predilection.

Because it is an elicited, analogic flow that expands point metaphor into frame metaphor, and a simple retroflexion of the latter that effects figure-ground reversal, the balance of life and death is similarly reversible. If I were speaking of a structure, a charter, an institution, or a constitution of course, this reversibility would be no problem. But obviation is carried forth by the analogic flow it elicits, not by the needs or interests of individuals or collectivities, or by bio- or socioenergetics, and so the danger of an inauspicious and unintended flow reversal is a very real and a very threatening one. Instead of relationship expanding outward into life process, death, for instance, would become contagious and threaten to "relate" its victims through the negativity of Souw's curse.

Except for instances of suspected or demonstrated sorcery, Daribi regard all illness or insanity as resulting from a "holding" or possession of the animating principle by the spirit of some specific deceased person. Illness, whether mental or physical, is in other words a metaphor of life through death and death through life: to the degree that a person suffers loss of faculties, the person is "dead," and to that same degree the ghost whose grievances or malevolence are manifested through the person's symptoms is "alive." Ghosts "live" through the persons they possess, and their victims, in the same measure, "die" through them.

The disposition of a ghost resulting from a "bad" death is particularly dangerous. The death of someone who succumbs in the bush, or whose body could not be recovered for mortuary purposes, is apt to spread as a contagion of illness and death among the pigs and children of the community. As these are, effectively, the means of ongoing relational flow, the threat is that of a possessional figure-ground reversal drawing the community itself to extinction. If such a threat is suspected and confirmed by signs, then the most complex and ambitious of traditional Daribi rituals, the *habu,* is performed. The full rite is complicated and time-consuming, engaging the efforts of a whole community for several months, and it is hedged around with prohibitions and potential hazards. Ostensibly performed in order to "bring the ghost back to the house," the *habu* can be seen as an effort to restore moral relations with the aggrieved spirit, and to prevent the contagion from claiming additional lives. It is in fact a *controlled* figure-ground reversal, intended to contain and forestall the uncontrolled one.

Like the myth of Souw, the *habu* gets underway in response to the cry of a bird, though in this case the bird is the *hogo'-bia*, or rufous shrike-thrush. This bird traditionally calls hunters' attention to the game drawn to a powerful plant known as *kerare*.[5] Here it is a form assumed by the ghost, which is bidding men to perform the *habu* on its behalf. Only if the cry of this bird is heard following an inauspicious death will the *habu* be undertaken. The bird's call should be answered with the *habu* "cry," a wailing call commencing with a rapid burring of the lips, to establish communication with the ghost and indicate a willingness to comply. The male population of the community then divide into the *habu* men and the house men *(be' habu)*, ritual adversary roles.

The *habu* men, generally young and often unmarried, must assume the costume and restrictions characteristic of the role; violation of these or other *habu* procedures will revert the metaphor of possession to an adverse one—a disastrous possession of the violators known as the "*habu* sickness." The *habu* men blacken the visible body with charcoal and wear a black cassowary plume on the head—exactly as in the *ogwanoma*, except that for the *habu* the white contrast is provided by large, silvery gray *Olearia* leaves worn across the forehead. They depart from the community to stay in the bush, where they will hunt and preserve game, and they "take the ghost with them." They must remain strictly celibate, and avoid all contact with women (and children) during their sojourn in the bush. In order to maintain communication with the ghost, the *habu* men should carry branches of the *kerare* plant with them (as the plant is thought to affect women adversely, only unmarried men should carry it).

The *habu* men live in small "*habu* houses" in the bush, and

5. *Kerare* is apparently related to, or identical with, the Polynesian *kava* plant, an intoxicant. It is related to another plant known to Daribi as *hogobi 'a*, almost homophonic with the bird's name.

they live there in a state of possession by the ghost—they "have the ghost on their skins." The spend their days hunting game and smoking the carcases (though snakes are taken and preserved *alive*); when game is encountered, they must give the *habu* cry and verbally reproach the creature, as it is killed or captured, for having caused illness in the community.

When a large quantity of game has been collected and smoked, the *habu* men are ready to return. Some of them go to the place where the death occurred and cry out to the ghost that they are ready to go back to the house. The ghost assumes the form of rain and wind, accompanied by a whistling sound, and follows the men and the "smell of the meat" back to the house. When they return, the *habu* men are still subject to possession by the ghost. In order to "prove themselves" to the ghost, and also to remove it from their skins, they must, on pain of the ghost's displeasure (the *habu* sickness), participate in ritualized opposition to the people of the house.

Upon their arrival at the garden surrounding the house, the men make a small shelter there, where they will stay until the ritual is concluded. As they arrive, and for a few days thereafter, they engage the house men in a form of energetic shoulder wrestling called *hwębo*. The jarring, violent activity can be said to absorb the force of the ghost's antagonism socially (and physically!); Daribi say it removes the ghost from the skins of the *habu* men. As a challenge to keep up the opposition to the house men, the *habu* men dance, carrying a wooden pole above their heads, into the main house, down its central corridor, and back out again.

While the *habu* men are arriving and initiating the bouts of *hwębo,* the women of the house (and often those of surrounding communities) appear in transvestite costume, as warriors, and they dance and sing to taunt the *habu* men. They beg to be given some of the smoked meat (which may not, of course, be shared with them). In addition to *hwębo* wrestling, the *habu* men engage in mock ambushes and skirmishes with the women who taunt them, each side flinging "spears" of peeled banana stalks into the houses of the other at night. The oppositional activity of wrestling, taunting, and skirmishing may continue for sev-

eral days, with the opposition of the women increasing as the
ritual progresses. It is interesting to note that the ritual is not
"enacted" from a "program" (as Westerners might do it) so
much as it is internally motivated through the competitive ener-
gies of the teams of performers. The tensions that are maintained, between the *habu* men and the house men, and between
the women and the *habu* men, are, moreover, scarcely arbitrary
"gimmicks" or introduced elements, for they correspond to the
elemental oppositions of the *habu* itself. Understood in its own
terms, the ritual is self-motivated.

After the ghost has been removed "from the skins" of the
habu men, the climactic phase of the ritual occurs—in the native
phrasing, it *darabo*, "flows to a head." The *habu* men remove
the smoked game from their small shelter (and kill the live
snakes) and pack it carefully into oversize net bags. The ostentatiously heavy loads are then lifted onto the backs of two
men (for each bag), with others supporting from the rear, and
borne in procession to the main house. The bags of meat are
escorted by the *habu* men, dancing in file and sounding re-
peatedly the burring of the lips associated with the *habu* cry.
The procession may circle in front of the house several times,
after which the bags are opened and the smoked meat is laid
out along the central corridor of the house. At this point several
sorts of revealing speeches may be given; generally there is
one by a member of the *habu* party explaining just why the
habu was done, and often naming the places where the game
was killed. Then a short, exculpating speech is made, blaming
the illness upon the smoked game, the "black" or "hand-
fastened" (referring to the wooden frame upon which the game
has been stretched in smoking it) "people." The ghost has now
been reconciled with the people of the community, its hostility
having been absorbed in the shock of *hwębo* wrestling, its attacks on pigs and children absolved through the reidentification
of the smoked game as agents. It remains now to dispose of
the game in what amounts to a realization of the mortuary feast
(traditionally a feast of game) that accompanies the course of
mourning.

The women, who have gathered, singing and dancing, in

ever increasing numbers, now begin "looking for banana trunks." As they find and peel the stalks, they will make repeated sallies against the house, holding the trunks above their heads. Eventually the force of their opposition gathers to a head, and they dance up the house ladder with the trunks in an attempt to carry them down the central corridor and throw them out the back door. Should they accomplish this, it is thought that "the souls of the men would go with them." Parties of men assemble at the rear door to prevent this, and the successive attempts are blocked with a wooden body shield. As the trunks are taken up by the men, chopped into pieces and scattered in front of the house, the *habu* comes to a close.

Its special status as a ritual, a metaphorical frame controlling the relation between two other metaphorical expansions, makes the *habu* something of a metaphor of a metaphor. Its obviation achieves neither a realization of convention via the exhaustion of image nor a realization of image through that of convention, but rather a rectification of the (metaphorical) interrelationship of convention and image. This means that it creates a metaphor of relationship through the myth of Souw's curse, and a metaphor of the curse of mortality through relationhip.

Each point in the *habu* sequence is a metaphor of the corresponding points in the relationship and mortality sequences. (Since the axial opposites *A–D, B–E,* and *D–F* are inverted between the two, as in fig. 13, a point metaphor in the *habu* sequence will amount to an expression combining axial opposites.) Each point, then, is constituted as a trope combining two expressions that are themselves metaphoric. But the cultural dialectic distinguishes between the two limiting conditions of metaphor, as image and as convention (or macrocosm and microcosm), as opposites. In these terms, the points that appear originally as conventions (*ACE* in the relationship sequence, *DBF* in the myth) will be metaphorized in the *habu* as images, whereas those that appear as images (*DBF* in the relationship sequence, *ACE* in the myth) will, as "metaphors of metaphors," be literalized in the *habu*.

The possession of pigs and children, respectively the adjunct and the complement of male contingency, that necessitates the *habu* is simultaneously a metaphorical interdiction of ongoing relationship via the "holding" of its means and its ends, and the literal "internalization" of an immortal agency—the ghost. (A Daribi ghost enters the liver in order to "hold" the animating principle.) *A,* then, substitutes the metaphorical "death" of illness for the metaphorical "life" of relationship by combining a figurative interdict (*A* in the relationship sequence) with a literal internalization of an immortal agency (*A* in the myth).

The *habu* will not be enacted, however, without the omen of the *hogo'bia* bird's cry—the ghost's call for the men to come and hunt game. But the rufous shrike-thrush does not "point out" active game, as does the *kaueri,* but creatures that have succumbed to the "holding" or possessive influence of the *kerare* plant's intoxicants. It is calling for men to hunt via the agency of possession, as *habu* men. Thus a metaphorical equivalent of the bird's cry in the Souw myth invokes a literalization of *B* in the relationship sequence: an "external" male flow in the form of *habu* men who leave their housemates and go out to the bush. And substitution *B* in the *habu* supplants the normatively social male/female opposition with a ritual male/male opposition of *habubidi* and *be' habu.*

As the hunters prepare to depart, they don a metaphorical *"ogwanoma"* with leaves substituted for pearl shells, a "wedding" is intended for the bush, at which the groom's party, rather than the bride, is "taken," and the "boy-soul" is given over (to the ghost's possession) rather than retained. Thus *C* in the relationship sequence is rendered metaphorical, and this is accomplished through the literalization of the metaphorical hunting of the snake at point *C* in the myth, for the *habu* men must foreswear sexuality and apply themselves to real hunting.

The *habu* men take the ghost away from the house, and are themselves "taken" or encompassed by the ghost that comes "onto their skins." This substitution, *D,* combines a literalization of the encompassment of conception (*D* in the relationship sequence) with a celibacy and separation (in the bush) from women that metaphorizes Souw's frustration and social detumescence in the myth. As a possession of the men themselves, in place of the adjuncts and products of male contingency, it resolves and cancels A.

Returning with the ghost "on their skins," and also surrounding them in the form of meteorological violence, the *habu* men bring the ghost back to the house and transmute the violence into a social encounter. *Hwębo* literalizes the "killing" of Souw's curse, and also the taking off of death with the skin manifested in Souw's "throwing down" of his skin (in the fact that the wrestling is said to dislodge the ghost from the skins of the *habu* men). It metaphorizes the normative *pagebidi* exchanges that both define one line of men against another and then relate them through matrilateral sharing. Thus, as the replacement of a social male/male schism with the cosmic one of ghost as against mortals, substitution E resolves and cancels B.

Attention now shifts to the morally appropriate focus of a ghost's concern: the meat of a mortuary feast. Substitution F effects the replacement of the *habu* men (and the ghost's culpability) by the game they have killed, a metaphor of the snakes' displacement of human beings at point F in the myth. As an offering up of the "black men" in place of the hunters' "*ogwanoma*" (and smoked meat is also a wedding gift), this metaphor releases them from their commitment to bush life, and cancels C. The coincident feast literalizes the sharing of meat between men of different lines (*hai'*), at point F in the relationship sequence, in the abundant sharing of meat between *habu* men and house men.

Sharing the complement of male contingency as a sacramental tribute to the dead obviates the ghost's possession of pigs and children at A: it restores the moral order between living and dead. But now the men are beset from a different quarter; the women, whose transvestite challenges have kept their performance on its mettle, now confront them directly. Their invasion of the men's quarters to capture and displace the men's souls (substitution G: women for men) both vindicates their transvestism and constitutes the "not-not" of substitution A. Like D, it involves the taking of the men's souls in place of the pigs' and childrens'; but, whereas in D this was accomplished in the bush by the ghost in the context of hunting animals, it is attempted here in the house by women wielding a plant cultigen. And it fails. In order to counter the women's threat, however, *habu* men and house men must form a united front, and, by negotiating a concerted male opposition to a concerted female effort, G effects a return to the normative gender opposition of Daribi secular life.

The fact that it "collapses" into neither macrocosm nor microcosm but into a relation between the two, makes the *habu* difficult to diagram. Although it takes the "generic" form of obviation, the *habu* cannot simply be represented by superimposing the diagram for the Souw myth onto that of the relationship sequence, for the relation of "encompassing" to "encompassed" points and triangles is opposite in the respective sequences. Because the inversion is such that the external triangle B–D–F of one is equivalent to the internal triangle A–C–E of the other, and vice versa, one of the sequences can be redrawn in inverted position, with A–C–E as the external points. If we then "fold" each diagram, the upright and the inverted, along its interior (dashed) lines, as in fig. 14, the external points of each can be joined to the corresponding internal points of the other to represent their metaphorical connection in the *habu*.

Thus the *habu* can be accurately diagrammed as a three-dimensional model, an octahedron (fig. 14) that includes the eight triangular faces of the two constituent sequences, but condenses their twelve points into the six of the generic obviation sequence. Instead of presenting the macrocosmic and microcosmic triangles in a relation of encompassment, the octahedral model shows them in a symmetrical relationship, as opposed but equivalent faces of the solid, with the movement of the sequence shuttling between them.

The octahedral model depicted in Figure 14 is every bit as holographic as the two-dimensional versions presented earlier; collapsed along its interior axes (by uniting point A with D, B with E, and C with F), it yields the *same* two-dimensional triangle as the standard (two-dimensional) obviation schema does when similarly collapsed. But there is a very significant difference between the two. For the octahedral model shows *two* "internal" or inscribed triangles, and if the reasons for constructing this sequence in three dimensions are valid, then this feature must have significance for motivation within the *habu*.

Performers in the *habu* are, in fact, motivated by two kind

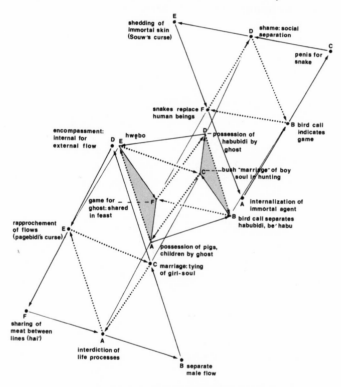

FIGURE 14: An octahedral model of the *habu*.

of "relativizing" forces, a situation familiar from ritual situations elsewhere in the traditional world. One is the cycle of retroactive implications that confronts the actor with the anticipated consequences of actions, familiar to the reader from the kin and mythic sequences considered previously. The other is a cycle of forward-moving implication, constraining the actor to carry forward each new stage in compliance with the stages already completed. This motivation can be identified with the intentions of the ghost, which *wants* the *habu* to be performed on its behalf (as the Daribi themselves point out). The ghost's intentions correspond to a *compulsion,* perceived by the *habu* men as external to their acting selves, but in fact integral to the obviative format of the ritual.

The motivating cycle of retroactive implication is concerned with gender relations and contingency. The ghost attacks pigs

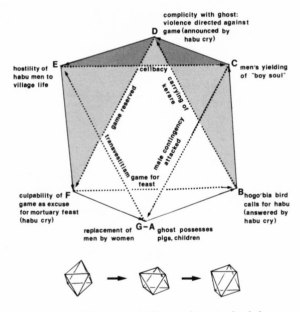

FIGURE 15: Motivation and compulsion in the *habu.*

and children, adjuncts of male contingency, as an implication of the men's yielding up their *ogwanoma'* to it (*C–A,* fig. 15), and to provoke them into doing so. The celibacy of the *habu* men as they go the the bush is an implication of their violent opposition to the *be' habu* and the village when they return (*E–C);* finally, the transvestism and provocative mockery of the *habu* men on the part of the women at *E* is an implication of their attempt to supplant the men and take their souls at *G*

(G–E). First the adjuncts of the men's reproductivity, then their sexuality, and finally their souls are threatened.

The compulsion to oppose this relativization is enacted in complicity with the ghost, and the *habu* cry is used to maintain communication. The cry is first given in response to the call of the *hogo ' bia* bird (fig. 15, *B*), whose "request" for game is a call for a mortuary feast in the context of the *habu,* and an implication of *F (F–B)*. As an earnest of their complicity, the men carry a *kerare* branch, and the cry is given whenever game is sighted and shot to establish concurrence with the bird's "request" (the implication of *B, B–D)*. The game is carefully treated, smoked, and preserved, and is also reserved by the *habu* men for use in the feast (it is this that the transvestite women challenge at *E,* as they sing allusive songs begging for a share of meat). At the culmination of the ritual, the cry is given again as the accumulation of preserved game is carried to the house, to shift the culpability for the attacks on the pigs and children onto it (and thus vindicate the implications of the killing at *D, D–F)*. Thus one and the same feast exculpates the ghost for its attacks and the men for having neglected its mortuary feast.

Both the cycle of retroactive implication and that of compulsion threaten the *habu;* the retroactive "relativization" by compromising a male activity through female introjection ("pollution"), the compulsive motivation by turning the metaphorical possession of the *habu* into the serious affliction of the *habu* sickness. The *habu* men are in this sense puppets, caught between two opposite relativizing forces in a kind of double-bind, and forced to work out the will of the ghost against the normative expectations of their social order (in this case, those of gender opposition).

Diagrams can be misleading as well as revealing. The *habu,* for all its three-dimensional intricacy, is not a "structure," except insofar as it structures a collapse or resolution. The Daribi, who respect and fear the *habu* sickness and all the contingencies of the ritual, rather accurately profess ignorance as to the significance of it all. Directly after I participated in the ritual, as a *habubidi,* at Tiligi' in 1968, I approached the man who had organized it on this matter. He and his clanmates were able to offer some penetrating insights, which have been incorporated in this analysis, but also claimed (characteristically) that the previous generation had died out without revealing the meaning of the whole. In fact, both the *habu* and the myth of Souw were consistently treated by the Daribi as secret knowledge, to be withheld from outsiders, and they never actively volunteered information concerning them.

Why is this nescience accurate? A trope or metaphor, whether formed of a symbolic reference point or as a larger cultural frame, remains cryptic. When an obviation sequence collapses into the paradox of a "not-not," it collapses its structure and its insights as well. The figure-ground reversal that motivates the Daribi construction of life (conception, sociality, relationship) and death, and that the *habu* holds in focus, is a captive paradox. It is effectively what David M. Schneider has termed a "core symbol." And it is also a matter of living human beings negotiating their lives through invisible and intangible termini, that can only be handled through metaphor and realized through its collapse. None of us, neither we nor the Daribi, has experienced death, or remembers the experience of birth, or has looked into the womb to see conception take place. *Others* are conceived and born, *others* die, and all that the collapsing, condensing trope of obviation can realize is the fleeting revelation of paradox become meaning in the "now" of its enactment, so that meaning may be resolved once again into paradox.

What is made problematic here is *time,* not so much in the creation of timeless "structures" determining temporal succession and performance (for we have seen what happens to these in obviation), as in the evanescent condensation of a world of meanings into the moment of its realization. Obviation balances the world upon the moment. Let us, then, consider this problematic.

5   Epoch: Real and Unreal Time

The three obviation sequences that have been considered occupy widely varying periods of "conventional" time in their working out. The cycle of kin relationship, if we wish to include the levirate among *hai'*, involves at least two generations, whereas the myth of Souw's curse can be narrated in a matter of minutes, and the *habu* requires something over a month or perhaps two for its completion. This contrast is all the more remarkable for the fact that it has little or no meaning in terms of constitution or interrelationship of the sequences themselves. What matters in the working out of a sequence, or in the transformation from one sequence to another, is a matter of relationship among points—opposition, mediation, cancellation—rather than arbitrary interval. However it may affect others, obviation defines and occupies its own time.

We might speak of this as "organic" or "mythic" time, for the events occurring within it have a definitive and nonarbitrary—in fact, an organic or constitutive—relationship to the sequence as a whole, as in the plot of a myth. Another way of putting this is that organic time does not accumulate (and *count*) like intervals; its events are in themselves relations, each one subsuming and radically transforming what has gone before. Each event, then, *differentiates* the character of the whole beyond anticipation, assimilating what has preceded it into its own relation, a "now" that supercedes, rather than extends, its "then." If the turn of phrase is helpful at all, I could speak of obviation as a qualitative mathematic, one that "uncounts" successive events, making itself a part of their resolution, rather than subordinating them to its order.

Bizarre as this concept may appear, the experience of an organic temporality should at least be somewhat familiar. It accounts for much of the "magic," literal and figurative, of myths and literary plots, and for many of the peculiarities of dreaming as well, for it is nothing more or less than the process of figurative expansion, the articulative resolution of meaning in large frames. Considered as "time," however, it contrasts so radically with the axiomatically universalized and naturalized tradition of conventional ("clock") time, that unless the underlying strains of assumption and implication are clarified, this analysis might incur accusations of social or scientific irresponsibility. Thus some searching questions about time are in order: Are there different *kinds* of time, or merely different ways of *counting* time? Does time have a structure, as a clock does, or does it merely seem to have a structure, *because* a clock has one?

It would seem as though anthropological approaches to time as cultural construct, including "genealogical time," the "time" produced by calendric combinations, and even the semihumorous self-referential time of ceremonies that happen only when they come to pass, deal largely with different ways of counting or describing time. The classical instance is Evans-Pritchard's notion of "structural time" (counterposed to oecological time, a system of culturally recognized environmental changes).[1] Structural time is developed through points of local group history and age-set and lineage reckoning, reducing time itself to social interval. Geertz's analysis of the Balinese permutational calendar, in "Person, Time, and Conduct in Bali," transforms the reckoning into a qualitative, rather than a quantitative, measure. The intermeshing of ten cycles of day names serves to *punctuate* or differentiate time into a fluctuation of varying socioreligious values that tell you, according to the author, not what time it is but what *kind* of time it is.[2] Such exceptions notwithstanding, the practice of calling different modes of counting time different cultural "times" is analogous

1. E. E. Evans-Pritchard, *The Nuer* (Oxford: Oxford University Press, 1940), 104–10.

2. Clifford Geertz, *The Interpretation of Cultures* (New York: Basic Books, 1973), 393 (see also footnote 31).

to calling systems that number according to different bases (sexagesimal, decimal, etc.) wholly different *mathematics*. It is not difficult to agree with Johannes Fabian that such studies of the cultural transformation of human experience remain sterile because of their inability "to relate cultural variation to fundamental processes that must be presumed to be constitutive of human Time experience."[3]

To say that our means of registering or reckoning something, *is* the thing reckoned, that the description is the thing described, is a familiar shorthand of everyday speech. It self-references our arbitrary "points of reference" within the necessities of speech and action, so that our acceptance of the conventional measure for the thing measured is virtually automatic. This is very much the case with "clock time," that of the calendar, of chronicles, and, therefore, of history, which we might call literal or referential time.

Whatever the means of measurement, literal time invariably represents its essence through spatial traverse (a clock, sundial, celestial arc, the tape on which atomic emissions are recorded, an electronic circuit), and it makes some sense, in this regard, to say that we measure space and call it time. (or, more precisely, we measure space as the "time" of our measurement.) Our grand symbols of temporality—the sidereal passages of heavenly bodies, the solar year, lunar configurations, the clock face, are spatial ones. Apart from the spatial analogies of gear-wheels, hourglasses, printed circuits, astronomical instruments, and the like, we have no means of representing temporal interval. What is more, we have no good empirical check, beyond the synchronization of other and different spatial analogies, on whether the "thing" that is being measured and analogized exists at all, much less whether it "flows" at the measured and uniform rate that our instruments suggest it does.

We measure time by injunction, simply asserting that that is what are clocks are doing. A clock or watch (or hourglass or any other chronological gadget) is merely a mechanism de-signed to operate at what we assume to be a uniform rate. The synchronization of these devices to realize "an accurate meas-ure of the passage of time" represents the extension and univ-ersalization of a conventional ideal rather than any sort of proof that the object of our measurement exists as a property of things. We do not measure or divine time so much as we "time" the measures themselves.

The "passage" of time is fairly obvious to everyone, the "presence" of time somewhat less so. But is this not because we measure, and therefore represent, time through its passage? Literal time is a shared value, and the reference of the shared value is to space, accumulation, plurality. As with other shared values, such as money or words, we might each "spend" it in different ways, or waste it. But it is entirely superfluous to ask, in this regard, how we can be sure that my two hours are the same as your two hours: as with all internalizations of the social and the collective, it is enough simply to assert that they are.

Is it worthwhile to speak of a personal or figurative time in contradistinction to the conventional? In a sense, the sense in which "time is money" or is *like* money, personal time is life, and the sum of life's rhythms, activities, and involvements that literal time gives a conventional valuation to. Insofar as it gives a very special "turn," a meaning or an inflection, to literal measure, drawing it into a "five-minute break," a "Thirty Years' War," or a "lifetime of foolishness," personal time can be treated as figurative. To the degree that it has a meaning and a center of its own, as autonomous biography, we can speak of it as organic time.

Life is in fact the only "kind" of time that we have, and literal time is a mere translation or common denominator of it. The things we do, through personal predilection or collective ethos (most generally a combination of these), give us the familiarity of temporal duration or presence. And it is because this experience, if it is worth anything at all, is *not* the experi-ence of measurement that a clockwatcher is familiar with, that clocks, watches, and sundials are necessary. As a bank does through money, or a dictionary through words, literal time transforms meaning into convention, and into the collective valuation that convention represents. And so life becomes time through the automatic internalization of collective necessity, and through the same ineluctable shorthand (or shortcut), time is imbued with the directionality of life.

Inasmuch as meaning (as perception) is the ground of our apprehension and understanding of things, any perception or representation of anything is achieved through meaning. And as obviation rings the changes of subject and object, figure and ground, through which meaning is constituted, I can add that a tropic perception or representation is achieved as the masquerading of meaning-flow *as* that thing. Thus the "life" that we exchange for time is no more ultimately a matter of biology or biography than the Daribi inversion of Souw's curse is a matter of external and internal "flow"; the real "flow" in both cases is a flow of analogy. Prehended meaning is organic time.

But organic time, as has been shown, subsumes its past within its present. The "life" that we give to conventional time in exchanging experience for measure is not duration—"passage"—but presence, like the immediate meaning of a trope. The content or "happening" of time is conventionally known as "event" or "incident." In the light of this discussion, however, both words connote too much subordination of presence to movement—too insignificant, like the tick of a clock—to be very helpful. I shall use instead the word *epoch* (from a Greek word meaning "stoppage" or "cessation"); this word is often used in contrast to the "interval" of time measurement. *Epoch* also connotes "turning point," and in this way accommodates the figurative notion of a "trope."

"Interval" is, after all, the very essence of using space to represent time, and an interval is measured by some kind of motion across a spatial traverse. The "stoppage" of epoch stands in contradistinction to this motion, for it constitutes a self-defined "piece" of time, something that is original and unmeasurable beyond all attempts at conventionalizing. Epoch, then, is time considered as organic, happening as one and the same as the frame within which it is perceived. Thus epoch is the fundamental factor in the differentiation of time; whereas space and velocity, the metaphors through which time is measured, give us our sense of relation and precision in time, epoch is the presence of time.

Like obviation, epoch is fundamentally impervious to the direction, movement, and subdivision of literal time; it is the trope of literal time—time that stands for itself. An epoch may be instantaneous or it may occupy eons; yet whether memory or classification assigns it to the past or future, its "time," as figurative realization, is always "now." And so epoch is time become consciousness, time as perception rather than as the perceived. It is always "now" because "now" is the immediacy of perception, whereas "then" is the alienation of the perceived.

If the presence of time can only be realized as a trope, a metaphor within the nontemporal means that we use to represent, to "measure," its passage, then time has no "structure," just as trope itself has none. The semblance of structure, or even complexity, as with metaphor itself or obviation, is entirely a consequence of a displacement of conventional points of reference. Time, like meaning, "happens" to convention.

But what of the "structure," the cyclicality, of literal time? Granting that epoch, assimilating all to its movement, its "now," admits of no measures or boundaries, we can ask how the measurement of time reaches a mediation between stasis and duration, between the "now" of the instant and the "then" of elapsed time. The answer is that this is achieved by circularity or recurrence, not only in the endless cycling of our twelve- or twenty-four-hour series, or in the rising and setting of celestial bodies, but also in the workings of the clock itself— its revolving gears or closing and opening circuitry. A return to the beginning point effectively nullifies the intervening motion and closes the cycle off into a unit. In this respect the cycles of literal time effectively simulate epoch, the closure of obviation. A cycle "passes" by closing.

But there is a crucial difference between the two. Because it is *not* trope or epoch, the clock's cyclical closure cannot *assimilate* past positions into a single expression, a "now." Although the intervening motion is nullified, the unit remains.

Thus, because it cannot obviate (because it cannot, in terms of my earlier turn of phrase, "uncount"), the clock (and the mode of reckoning that it supports) *accumulates* closures as *countable* units, it generates *plurality,* the modality of number and space.

If the "now" of epoch constitutes the unit of time and consciousness, then the accumulation of unresolved closures as plurality amounts to the deflection or alienation of epoch. We *measure* time, then, through the alienation of number, by, as Bergson put it,

> substituting for the concrete reality or dynamic progress, which consciousness perceives, the material symbol of this progress when it has already reached its end, that is to say, of the act already accomplished together with the series of its antecedents.[4]

The world of spatially constructed time has no center, no "now," for its (self-contained) present must always be represented through a counterposed medium that diverts and decontextualizes it. The immediacy of time as an encompassing realization is lost in the act of rendering it onto a representational medium. What we see on the dial of a clock is only incidentally a product of the act of looking; it is in fact the result of a mechanical productive process of the clock itself. *Now* is thus systematically sublimated off and redefined as a function of complex numerical relationships; it becomes a "then," an "other" moment, an anticipation of happening on the order of past moments, and thus an anticipation of the past. As long as the reference point of our experience of time, and our understanding of time, is located elsewhere, as long as it is *located* at all, time will be cheated of its "now" and its meaning.

The self-contained quality of time is its "happening," but the other-reference of space always locates a "here" with reference to "there." The plurality of space, which Bergson

4. Henri Bergson, *Time and Free Will: An Essay on the Immediate Data of Consciousness,* trans. F.L. Pogson (London: George Allen & Co., 1912), 190.

equates with the quality of number, amounts to a kind of equivalence among points such that each is always simultaneous with, or even substitutable for, the others. But "happening" is irreversible, and hence mortal: an epoch recalled is already part of another epoch.

In his studies of (Swiss) children's cognitive development, the psychologist Piaget has introduced the concept of "reversibility" as a property of what he calls "operational thinking." Paraphrasing his own description, "reversibility" characterizes the imaginative capability that treats and analyzes its subjects as distinct and integral entities, independent of the act of imagining them. Reversible thinking allows us to (cognitively) make allowance for the independent existence of objects, to "conserve" shapes and volumes, and to generalize on such properties. Thus reversibility is a feature of spatial and mathematical conceptualization, an ability, clearly, to conceive of and sustain uniquely realistic and consistent worlds.

Our notion of "space," as it emerges distinct from "time," is certainly a product of reversibility. Space is accorded an objective integrity, and the time that is used up in perceiving, tracing out, measuring, or otherwise figuring it does not affect its objectivity. Time, however, even the successiveness of organic time, belongs unquestionably to the irreversible. "Here" is a place you may have visited in the past, and might return to in the future, but "now" does not have this property. Thus the suggestion might be ventured that space and time are, respectively, reversible and irreversible analogues of one another.[5]

Time must be "frozen" into space, made reversible, in order to be counted, to be figured as a countable plurality. And so a unit of space, or of a spatial analogue of time, is a modeling of the perceived world, objectified independently of the act of imagining it. Epoch, as the model of the perceiving consciousness, time *as* the act of imagining, is not only classifiable as organic time, it is, so to speak, "coterminous" with it. Organic time, its representations in trope and obviation, and, therefore,

5. Ibid., 100.

meaning, are examples of epoch, the only time we experience directly, and the only mode we have for experiencing time directly. Epoch *is* time; literal time is the representation of time through its own alienation.

The implications of this must be insisted upon, for they are not a part of our conventional sense of time. Because epoch, the "now" that is the only time there has ever been or ever will be, is the point of perception or consciousness, it constitutes time organically. What we call, on the model of literal time reckoning, "past" and "future" times, are equally emergent impingements on the "present," since *anything additional that I may learn or recall about the past as well as my recollection of anything I already "know" about the past, lies in the future of what I now call the "present."* Important as the discrimination between past and projected, or imagined, happenings certainly is to the mind's orientation, all of them are equally superadded to the situation at hand. Thus memory and invention, or creation, are both species of projection, imaging forth metaphorical transformations of a "known" order upon the foreground of a moving "present." Because we rely on memory, expectation, and aspiration to give continuity to our thoughts and actions, it follows that we live the sequences of our lives *backward* and *forward* from every epochal moment. Every instant is the beginning of the past. As Bergson put it:

> Outside of me, in space, there is never more than
> a single position of the hand and the pendulum,
> for nothing is left of past positions. Within my-
> self a process of organization or interpretation, of
> conscious states is going on, which constitutes
> true duration.[6]

Past and future are but images, transformations or transpositions of an equally projective image called the "present,"[7]

6. Ibid., 108.
7. "Now" is a trope because literal simultaneity is impossible; the experience of *now* as the immediacy of thought corresponds to the formation of a trope "between" the immediate past of a just-now realized perception, and the anticipation of intention. By the time a situation is perceived it is already past;

and every bit as metaphorical. A memory of childhood, an episode from the Middle Ages, or a fantasy of the near or distant future: each is a piece of figurative time that belongs to a flow of analogy—a "now" that remembers or imagines itself into (and out of) other "nows." Though one might "time" the subject with a stopwatch (as sleepers are monitored in dream laboratories), this flow of analogy has nothing to do with the passage of clock time: its necessity is neither that of a parade of inexorably precise seconds and nanoseconds in slavish imitation of our measuring devices, nor of a cosmos in majestic but inexplicable motion though a "fourth dimension." It has to do with the self-sealing and nonnegotiable quality of epoch as organic time.

The spatialization of time is more obvious in modern Western civilization than in any other; often it seems as though our powerful telescope mirrors were intended to *deflect* cosmic epoch to the farthest possible reaches. Our cosmogonic cycles— the creation and dissolution of the material universe—are pushed out to the limits of remote processes of spatial evolution, like dim astronomical parentheses enclosing our history and much more besides. Within this space a uniform and abstracted time ticks by, unpunctuated by apocalypse or Meso-American calendric holocausts. What others would perceive as epoch is dissociated by an unconscious disavowal of the link between time and human perception.

Space, the modeling of the perceived, has no element of immediacy to be dissociated from; we can see as far into space as we are able. But epoch is delimited practically by human and mortal capabilities; it is "organic" time in a double sense— human life and mortality as well as the conflation of event and medium. The modeling of a perception extending "from the Cretaceous to the present" implies something fairly prodigious in terms of mortal capacity: what kinds of life processes and

---

thus the world we see and hear is not the one we act in. We "throw" ourselves blindly into our actions, guided only by a learned anticipation of what is "out there" based on experience. "Now" is an experience that welds perception and intention into an image (and illusion) of simultaneity.

life experiences would have to accompany such an epoch? Because the living consciousness is definitive of time, the scale expansion is not at all the same sort of thing as extrapolating familiar distances into light-years. And yet it is accomplished with the same facility as magnifying subatomic particles of evanescent duration into universal problems, or reducing swarms of galaxies to clusters of miniscule particles on a photgraphic plate.

From the standpoint of trope and meaning-constitution, the orienting frame of this discussion, cosmic or astronomical time amounts to a mystical infusion of human capabilities into the fabric of reality, like Eddington's notion of the universe as a "thought in the mind of God." Understood as a metaphor in itself, a mystical infusion (no more and no less than man's original immortality, or Souw's immortal skin, in Daribi myth), it compels an imaginative world of tremendous scope and Faustian power. The trope is formed, as are all tropes, in the "now" of its realization, and the astronomer who formed it will die, perhaps, before the flash of his cigarette lighter reaches the edge of our spiral arm, but the *sense* of the trope is a godlike perception that spans millennia.

Approached as the subject or content rather than the *condition,* of a trope, spatialized time has the scale-changing effect of other astronomical instruments. But the evidence suggests that spatialization and analytic magnification are pervasive beyond the confines of astronomy. It is noteworthy that Fabian, who correctly accuses theorists of the "cultural construction" of time of ignoring its constitutive aspects, does so as part of his general critique of the use of time to estrange and objectify the "other" in anthroplogy.[8] Time is misconstrued, first of all, as if it were the space by which we measure it, and second as if it were an interval separating anthropologist and subject. Thus the likelihood arises that the spatialization of time is a part of what we could call a general topological distortion in the Western worldview, one that lies at the root of our mis-

8. Fabian, *Time and the Other,* chap. 5.

understanding of trope as well. It is scarcely a coincidence that the Western science of meaning, semiotics, was founded upon the severing of the sign from perceptual image.

The clock, the calendar, and the chronicle do not express or image the "contents" of happening; rather, they "measure" them via arbitrary numbers that represent the accumulation of empty and unresolved cyclical closures. Rationalist science and technology extend this measurement of an inscrutable "happening" to its representation and replication through the plurality of unresolved closure, through number, numerical function, and reciprocating mechanical or electronic cycle. Thus the practical basis of rationalist civilization and its ideals is the *simulation* of epoch, and of resolution, mortal closure, and meaning, through contrived and arbitrary but controllable means.

The significant locus of this "capture" and replication of "natural" cyclicality for Western civilization was the mechanical clock, initially developed by De Dondi and others as a simulator of celestial movements. The core of the innovation, the escapement mechanism (also known from an earlier Chinese device, a huge wooden eclipse predictor used by the emperor), effects the retardation, the self-checking or obviation, of cyclicality by its own movement. Checking or retarding the movement is a means of controlling it, and control is the single advantage to be gained by replication. Because an analogous control is necessary in the decentering of energy from the epoch of its happening that propels every machine, the simulated epoch of "time" and the simulated epoch of "work" have a common ancestor in the clock. As Lewis Mumford has observed:

> The clock, not the steam engine, is the key machine of the modern industrial age. . . . In its relationship to determinable quantitites of energy, to standardization, to automatic action, and finally to its own special product, accurate timing, the clock has been the foremost machine in modern

technics . . . it marks a perfection toward which
other machines aspire.[9]

For those who would attribute "natural" qualities of power
or force to our automatic technology, the steam engine is an
obvious choice for the ancestral machine. Historically (in its
inauguration of the English industrial revolution) as well as
practically, the steam engine symbolizes that most socio-
morphic of mechanical attributes, work. But the clock came
first,[10] and, given the specific considerations Mumford men-
tions, it is questionable whether the steam engine could have
been conceived in effective form had the clock not preceded it.
Indeed, piston for pendulum or mainspring, governor for escapement, the steam engine is a kind of clock, one that keeps
its "time" with a considerable pragmatic authority. Much the
same can be said of its petroleum- or electricity-powered de-
scendants; every automatic machine is a "clock."

The more modern electronics industry (mechanics with an
inbuilt "perception") employs circuit closure as a highly flex-
ible "internal wheel," with a usefully negotiable closure. Wheel
and circuit technology, in its modern development, belongs to
the special genius of Western culture, and its pragmatic application of the dialectic, concealed behind the sleek contours of
an automobile body or the winking facade of a computer,
makes it possible for the culture to use the dialectic without
ever having to own up to its wider implications.

Ostensibly a harnessing of natural force to serve cultural
ends, technology is in fact a harnessing of culture, a decentering
and "domestication" of the reflexivity of trope that fuels cultural motivation. By the same token, natural science might be
seen as the application of technology to explanation, modeling
the workings of the universe by creating functional and "tool"
explanations, rebuilding the subject of study analogically as if

9. Lewis Mumford, *Technics and Civilization* (New York: Harcourt Brace,
1959), 14–15.
10. Jean Gimpel, *The Medieval Machine: The Industrial Revolution of the Middle
Ages.* (New York: Holt, Rinehart and Winston, 1976), 152–54.

it were a machine—producing the universe as a model of production. At the core of this ambitious effort is the mystique that identifies a description or an imitation of self-contained efficacy with "nature." We say that the laws or forces of nature are at work in our machines or formulas (and that the principles of our technology can be observed in nature), that technology harnesses and science reveals an innate natural order, and so contrive a felicitious cosmic sanction for our practical symbology.

The problem is that the "nature" represented through such mechanistic analogies is a physicist's description of nature, an abstract and mathematical model of natural order itself conceived in mechanical terms on the assumption that nature operates more or less like a machine. Though it is not difficult to find evidences in natural phenomena of the conversion or conservation of energy, the models to which the evidence is addressed have been provided by our technology. Thus, since the conversion and conservation of energy are primarily exemplified by technological experience, the "nature" symbolized in a machine is essentially the nature of technology. Machines work as nature would work if nature were a machine.

A world of thought and action that is oriented by arbitrary convention, historical time and rationalized relations—decentered epoch—has not estranged itself from nature (the product, and the illusion, of its estrangement), but from culture. It is, as Richard Sennett has correctly diagnosed, *symbol* (in its constitutive form of trope, and as constitutor of a social world) that is problematic. And so the major articulative industry of modern civilization is interpretive, the effort to recenter epoch and trope as meaningful and productive elements in personal, intellectual, and commercial life. Culture and symbol must be invented: through hermeneutics, phenomenology, anthropology, history, literature, and literary criticism academically, and through advertising, entertainment, the "news" and commentary on the news—the "national conversation," popularly. We invent culture for others because we are in the business of inventing one for ourselves.

The interpretive industry is secondary in relation to the

primary industry of molding a technical and rational world from decentered epoch, but it is primary from the standpoint of the inhabitants of that world, whose meanings, as well as products, are alienated. The invention of culture is motivated by the invention of nature. It is the familiar plight of urban civilization overextended, of the Roman rhetoric in theory and practice, the Aztec phenomenology of trope and metaphor of which Leon-Portilla writes, and, finally, of Spengler's "second religiosity"—Sufism, and the Buddhist "pure light of the void."

Is the obviation of obviation a historical consequence? Is it, perchance, a product of obviation itself? Let us consider the Western case in historical perspective.

6   The Western Core Symbol

Berengar, scholasticus of Tours and archdeacon of Angers, the most brilliant pupil of the famous Fulbert of Chartres, was a student of grammar and rhetoric and a gifted Latin versifier of the eleventh century. Skilled also in dialectics, he is best known for his affirmation and stubborn defense of the figurative nature of the Christian eucharist. His position was officially condemned as heretical, and he was forced to recant again and again; yet the acuity of his arguments was remembered, and later writers, like John Wycliffe, often sought to vindicate him. It is not for this reason, however, that I begin with him, but simply because, like the contemporary anthropologist David M. Schneider, but at a very different time and for very different reasons, he called attention to what we can speak of as a cultural "core symbol."

Clearly, of course, Berengar's symbolic eucharist is by no means the same thing as the conjoining of law and nature (code for conduct and substance) that organizes American kin relations (and, indeed, Amercan culture as a whole) in Schneider's writings. Both are, however, concerned with the mediation of basic dualities, and both, in a more specific sense, are concerned with the transformation of blood and substance. Given that they belong to the same traditional continuity, we might consider the possibility of their interrelationship. How might they figure in the expansion of point metaphor to cultural frame that constitutes the Daribi core symbolization?

The theoretical implications of this question have to do with the versatility and usefulness of the obviation model of trope expansion: Is it applicable to the core symbolization of a civilization, or "high culture," as well as to that of a people like the Daribi? If so, what can its application tell us about the similarities and differences between these two ostensibly dissimilar kinds of tradition?

If we begin with Berengar's eucharist as the trope of a mediation of the hierarchical relation of God and man (much as the expansion of the Daribi core symbol began with the trope

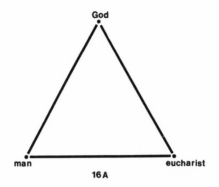

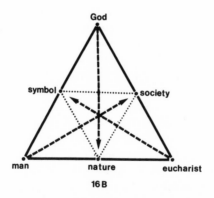

FIGURE 16: The core mediation of Latin Christendom.

of *ge*), we can construct the familiar mediative triangle (fig. 16A). The notion of a sacramental meal, or partaking of substance, as a mediative linking of human and divine has its roots in early Judeo-Christian tradition. Gillian Feeley-Harnik traces this early notion to two assumptions:

The first is that the food God provides is his
word; the food embodies his wisdom. The second
is that eating God's wisdom should establish a
binding agreement, a covenant, among the eaters
to abide by his word.[1]

For Berengar, and for the Christians who preceded and followed him, "eating God's wisdom" in this way implied, *in some
form or other,* a divine presence identifiable with Jesus Christ as
the (sacrificial) mediator between God and man, and, by extension, with the church that represents Christ via its succes-
sorship to the See of Peter. (The commonest medieval formula
equating Christ with the divine presence spoke of "Jesus Christ
who . . . sits at the right hand of God.") Figure 16A, then, represents the basic mediative formulation of medieval Latin
Christendom.

If a median line is dropped from each point of the mediation
to the opposite side, as in figure 16B, an obviational format is
generated. If we identify the cross-axial opposite of each point
of the original mediation with the *object* of the entity or agency
it represents (as God created *natura* as his object, man created
society), then the obviation becomes one of creative antitheses.
An inscribed, internal mediation is set up in which each point
on the internal triangle mediates between two on the external,
and vice versa. Thus "society," the object of man, mediates
between God and the eucharist as the clerical/secular hierarchy
through which the divine presence is conferred. "Nature," the
object of God, mediates between man and the sacrament via
the raw materials of grain and fermented juice transformed and
consumed in the eucharist. The symbolic juncture of society
and nature, registered as "symbol" in Figure 16B, mediates
between God and man as the biblical *logos,* or divine word, and
as the medieval concept of divine grace *(gratia).*

Considering the internal or inscribed triangle as a mediation
in its own right, as the mediation of nature and society by
symbol, it is clear that this "opposite" of the eucharistic me-

1. Gillian Feeley-Harnick, *The Lord's Table: Eucharist and Passover in Early
Christianity* (Philadelphia: University of Pennsylvania Press, 1981), 82.

diation is equivalent to the epitomizing, or core, symbolic mediation of Schneider's *American Kinship*. Thus the identifications of basic symbols made, at different times, under entirely different circumstances, and for different reasons, by Berengar of Tours and David M. Schneider, are in fact the respective "inside" and "outside" of each other; they are, in every sense of the Daribi inversion, a figure-ground reversal.

If this is the case, then, like Louis Dumont's *homo hierarchicus* and *homo aequalis,* the hierarchical medieval eucharist and Schneider's egalitarian epitomizing symbol each contains the other within it, if only by implication. Both are equally present within the medieval and modern periods, but as the respective formulations of Berengar and Schneider indicate, they are "present" in respectively different ways. This suggests, then, that the figure-ground reversal of Western civilization is *temporally* or historically, rather than ritually, articulated.

A ritualized articulation of a figure-ground reversal is exemplified by the Daribi *habu,* which controls the threatened reversibility of the respective frame metaphors of life process and mortality by enacting a ritual resolution that encompasses both simultaneously. A temporal articulation would involve the historical enactment of the reversal itself, by obviating first one "side" (as internal "resistance") of the inverse figure through the other, and then reversing the process. That some such inversion or transformation of a religious into a secular orientation took place, roughly at the time of the Reformation, has been widely suggested. Perhaps its most familiar articulation has been Weber's *The Protestant Ethic and the Spirit of Capitalism.*

But a caveat is necessary here. The temporal or historical obviation of a core symbol, however intrinsically important it may be in historical development, is an idealogical process. It is by no means to be identified or confused with history itself— the "actuality" of event and personality—and it would be a mistake to imagine that it either explains or determines history. History, in the fullest sense in which its "actuality" is conceived by modern scholarship, suffers neither explanation nor determination. As with the subjects of anthropological field investigation, however, certain aspects of it can be effectively modeled, and if the limitations of the model are kept in mind, a limited advantage can be realized also.

In the modeling of a core symbol, and its figure-ground reversal, we are concerned with meaning. This is a limited interest, with parallels in the work of Louis Dumont and David Schneider, and must be sharply distinguished from historical models of ideals and institutions (politics, constitutional history) on one hand, and those of practical and material considerations (development, economic history) on the other. Both ideally and practically based models have a vested interest in historical accretion and continuity, in the idealogical "progress" of this "-ism," freedom, or institution, or the flourishing of that city, social class, or profession. The advantage of an ideological modeling is that, being dialectical and recursive, it can supply a formal corrective to the linear and content-oriented traditional models.

Time as constitutive epoch, my central concern in this model, has no necessary equivalence with historical or chronological time. But an epochal figure-ground reversal that is articulated temporally—through the flow of history—might be expected to show some resonance with the time of calendar and chronicle. Thus, although I shall use epochs rather than dates or celebrated events as the points of obviative analysis, they can be expected to correspond fairly evenly with the chronological mapping of Western history.

The position on the eucharist that Berengar maintained against concerted opposition in church councils from 1050 to 1079 had its roots in an earlier confrontation, which A. J. Macdonald, author of the classic work on the subject, calls the "first eucharistic controversy."[2] (Berengar's was the second.) The notion of the figurative nature of the eucharist represented the teachings of Saint Augustine, and seems to have constituted the predominant interpretation of the sacrament from the Carolingian period until Berengar's time.[3] It was challenged, however, by Paschasius Radbert, abbot of Corbie in the reign of

2. A. J. Macdonald, *Berengar and the Reform of Sacramental Doctrine* (London: Longmans, Green, and Co., 1930), 231.
3. Ibid., 237–38.

Charles the Bald (831), who argued for the "metabolist" position of Saint Ambrose, that the content of the eucharist is the true flesh and blood of Christ.

Almost immediately, Radbert's interpretation was countered by another monk of Corbie, Ratramnus. In a work commissioned by Charles the Bald, Ratramnus wrote that the sacrament was only mentally and relatively the body and blood of Christ. But the most profound and comprehensive work of the time, and the one that seems to have nurtured Berengar's own ideas, was *De divisione naturae,* by the Irish monk and philosopher John Scotus Erigena (810–77). In this work the whole of nature, as God's creation of himself in manifest form, is understood as a sort of figurative sacrament. God's substance, according to Erigena, cannot be known except insofar as it is figuratively reflected or manifested in nature. Man, created in God's image, reflects all things in nature and is the *copula mundi,* the universal catalyst, so to speak.

Erigena's philosophy of pantheism as sacrament, and sacrament as pantheism—nature as God's creation of himself, a view sanctioned by the orthodox Augustinian interpretation of the times—marks the beginning point *(A)*, of the obviation of the Western core symbol. Its epoch, that of the first emperors of Latin Christendom, embodies the first serious West-European consideration and disputation of the Eastern religious mystery.

Berengar, who upheld this Augustinian view, was destined to be the major dissident of his era, as Radbert, with his Ambrosian doctrine, had been of the Carolingian. Berengar's, in the late eleventh century, was the epoch of the reform papacy of Gregory VII, who had humiliated the Holy Roman Emperor Henry IV in the snows of Canossa over the issue of the investiture of bishops. Perhaps a militant church that asserted the right to install its own officials demanded a nonderivative sacrament as well ("If hitherto we hold only the figure, when shall we have the thing itself?" cried an outraged deacon, regarding Berengar's position, at the Council of Vercellia in 1050).[4] Hil-

4. Ibid., 81.

debrand, the principal author of the reform, who became Pope
Gregory VII, had earlier shown Berengar the sympathy of one
reforming spirit for another, and even as pope sought to protect
him from the mobs of his detractors (though he came within
hours of subjecting Berengar to the ordeal of the hot iron in
November of 1078).[5] Eventually, for his own as well as Berengar's safety, he was obliged to force Berengar to recant.

The epoch of Gregory VII and the wakening papal reform
was committed to the reality of the eucharistic transformation;
it sought a miracle where the earlier age had found a mystery.
This is manifest in the statement that Berengar was forced, by
an extremely hostile assembly, to read before them in Rome
(1059):

> That the bread and wine which are placed on the
> altar, after consecration are not only a sacrament,
> but the true body and blood of our Lord Jesus
> Christ, and perceptibly not only in the Sacra-
> ment, but in reality, are touched and broken by
> the hands of the priest and ground by the teeth
> of the faithful.[6]

Thus a literalization, or acceptance as reality, of the figurative
Augustinian sacrament of the Carolingian period can be counted as the second substitution, point B, of the medieval sequence.
It coincides with the investiture controversy and the assertion
of the right of the Holy See to invest its own officials, as against
their blatant political appointment by secular lords, which had
been the practice since before Charlemagne (whom Spengler
calls the "Caliph of Frankistan") had assumed the title "Pro-
tector of the Faithful."

As a mediation between the domineering "protectorship"
of the early lords and the fierce automony asserted by Hildebrand, on one hand, and the Augustinian figurative and Ambrosian literal sacraments on the other, the subsequent epoch

5. Ibid., 189.
6. Ibid., 130–31.

was a remarkable one. It substituted a socially reformed church—a religious "society" of orders and monasteries—and a kind of religious episociety of crusader states in the Levant and Papal States in Italy for the earlier secular proprietorship and the Hildebrandian doctrine of purity that followed. And it substituted a burgeoning scholasticism—often called the "twelfth-century renaissance"—of open, reasoned disputation for Carolingian intuition and for the anti-intellectual literalism of the previous epoch. The epoch of the early to mid 1100s, point C, or the first closure, of the medieval obviation, was a medieval discovery of society and reason.

The societization of religion was not to slacken its pace until the Fourth Lateran Council of 1215 forbade the founding of new orders. Its obsession with ethos can be seen in the life and writings of its most famous exponent, Bernard of Clairvaux, and in the widespread concern with monastic rules. But a code for religious conduct, however societal the community, is not necessarily a tolerant one. Rational disputation is social or public thought, and universities, which began their rise in this era, might be described as the societization of reason or inquiry. Inevitably, as had Hildebrand in the previous epoch, Bernard came into conflict with the spirit of inquiry—in the person of Peter Abelard. Abelard had posited, purely for argument's sake, a number of heretical propositions in a treatise on the Trinity, and Bernard led those who condemned it and drove him out of public life.

But in terms of sacramental conceptualization the significant development of the age was scholastic, not monastic. Whereas earlier commentators on the sacrament from Radbert to Berengar approached the subtances of the sacrament—the wine and bread—in a straightforward manner, as things that either did or did not change, the realists and nominalists of the twelfth century could make nice distinctions between essences and accident, or between the word and the thing signified. Thus the opposition between figurative and literal interpretations was mediated by a conceptual subtlety in dealing with symbolization. Gilbert de la Porree, for instance, of the School of

Chartres, argued for the separation of (Platonic) universals, such as divinity, from the accidental properties that accompanied them.

The epoch that followed, point D by this reckoning, is most often taken as the high point of medieval achievement. It coincides with the papacy of Innocent III, a hierarchical ordering of the powers of Latin Christendom beneath the authority of the pope that approached theocracy, and the Fourth Lateran Council, which made the sacramental doctrine of transubstantiation a dogma. This was also the era of Thomas Aquinas and of the refinement of Gothic architecture.

The doctrine of transubstantiation was developed from the realist philosophy of the previous epoch, and was based on the assumption of the essential reality of conventional conceptual or verbal categories. The imperceptible type-essence, or universal, inherent in every particular thing according to its kind, was called the *substantia*. The sensuous, perceptible aspects that differentiate the thing from others of its generic were called *accidentia*. On this basis,

> the idea of transubstantiation is that in the consecration of the elements the *substantia* change but the *accidentia* remain the same. The *substantia* of the bread and wine become the *substantia* of the body and blood of Christ. The *accidentia* remain the same, and the *accidentia* are all that remain of the original bread and wine.[7]

This made the ground of being, the divine presence in communion with clergy and worshipers, a kind of disembodied trope, like a figure of speech moving independently of language. (The idea itself is mystical, like Newton's "direct action at a distance," or the modern entropy.) But if the transformation was mystical and formless, its product was nonetheless, as *substantia,* conventional. Here again, as in *B,* a basically tropic expression becomes substantive, by virtue of being identified as miracle, and as superordinate reality.

7. William Barclay, *The Lord's Supper* (London: SCM Press, 1967), 72.

Nothing could stand in greater contrast than this to Erigena's conception of the natural world, the *accidentia*, as the figure or manifestation of God. And so the doctrine of transubstantiation cancels the Carolingian figurative sacrament as effectively as the theocratic papacy of Innocent III reversed the secular domination of the church under Charlemagne. Figure 17 develops this evolution of the Western sacrament in the conceptual terms of transubstantiation. The initial Augustinian

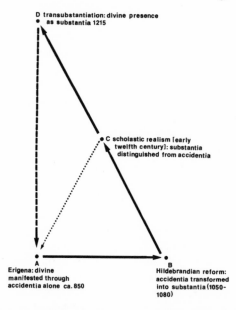

FIGURE 17: Sacramental evolution in scholastic terms.

doctrine, as articulated by Erigena, conceived of the divine presence as a *figura*, an iconic manifestation through the *accidentia* of nature alone. The Hildebrandian reformers, at *B, equated* this figure of *accidentia* with the *substantia* of the divine presence, so that the eucharist enacted the miracle of *accidentia* become *substantia*. The following epoch, *C,* negotiated the philosophical distinction between *substantia* and *accidentia,* and the Fourth Lateran Council, at *D,* recognized the divine presence in the sacrament as *substantia*.

It was Innocent III who identified the office of the pope as that of the "vicar of Christ on earth," and that exalted conception dominated the tenor of papal claims throughout the thirteenth century. It became even more grandiose with the accession of Benedetto Caetano to the papal throne as Boniface VIII at the end of the century. At this point we enter the epoch of the collapse of the medieval "papal monarch" as a dominant unifying force in Latin Christendom. In part, Boniface might be said to have accelerated the collapse by his stubborn resistance to the French king Philip the Fair and other grasping secular rulers of his day, though the claims of his office placed him in an impossible position. He responded, however, by upping the ante: in his bull *Unam Sanctam* (1302), he asserted infallibility and the right to depose monarchs, and concluded: "We declare, proclaim, and define that subjection to the Roman pontiff is absolutely necessary to salvation for every human creature." (He died in 1303 after a kidnapping attempt by Nogaret, an agent of Philip the Fair.)

Boniface is credited with raising the papal tiara to the height of an ell, and adding two crowns to it. More importantly, for the purposes of this study, he devised in 1300 a kind of sacred writ called an indulgence, which, if granted, would absolve a confessed, forgiven, and repentant person from the temporal punishment of purgatory. In granting this writ (in return for a monetary donation), the church drew upon the store of merit laid up with God through Christ's sacrificial death on the cross. Indulgence had been granted earlier by popes, and the idea of a store of divine grace or merit was articulated by Saint Anselm in his book *Cur Deus Homo?*, written in an earlier epoch (1097–99). But the large-scale dispensing of grace, a sacramental product, by the church for its own purposes, which commenced at Boniface's grandiose papal jubilee in 1300, is a matter that bears upon our main theme. It was a kind of spiritual equivalent of the *fief-rente,* a contemporary practice of substituting a money payment for the personal services required of a vassal.

The granting of indulgences was based on the church's access to the merit acquired for man by the death of Christ, and on the church's (exclusive) authority to dispense it. In this regard the practice may be linked to the extreme claims for papal authority and exclusiveness voiced in Boniface's bull *Unam Sanctam.* It manifested a kind of capitalism and contractualism of divine grace. From the standpoint of the church, in fact, it amounted to a kind of *production* of donations, with the merit of Christ's sacrifice as capital. As substitution *E,* it represents the negation and cancellation of the literalized Hildebrandian sacrament, for whereas in the early sacrament the church ministered to the transformation of the *accidentia* of bread and wine into the *substantia* of the divine presence, the granting of indulgences ministered to the transformation of the *substantia* of divine grace into the *accidentia* of monetary or other worldly donations. The church was *economically* produced through divine grace.

The theory of indulgences was articulated in the *Unigenitus* of Pope Clement IV in 1349,[8] and the notion on which it was based had widespread ramifications in the public fancy. One of these led to the millenarian cult of the heresy of the Free Spirit, medieval "hippies" who lived as they pleased in the belief that Christ had laid up an infinite store of merit, which was accessible to everyone without clerical ministration. Heresies of this sort were inevitable once the church set itself up, as it had in the epoch of Boniface VIII, as the exclusive dispenser of spiritual privileges in the afterlife. As the "vicar of Christ on earth" the pope had arrogated to himself divine agencies, supplanting the divine presence as the mediator between God and man. Writs of indulgence did not, in themselves, effect the remission of sin, but only represented the church's intercession for the reduction of purgatorial penitence. Nor were these writs in themselves by any means as significant for church or laity as the eucharist. But the position assumed by the church in producing itself economically through exclusive access to divine grace—its transformation of *substantia* into *accidentia*—shifted attention from the nature of the divine presence to that of its human ministration.

8. Adolf Harnack, *Outlines of the History of Dogma,* trans. E. K. Mitchell (Boston: Beacon Press, 1957), 484.

The epoch of Boniface VIII marks the second closure, at E, of the medieval obviational cycle. Negating the sacramental doctrines of Lanfranc of Bec and Guitmund of Aversa in the Hildebrandian era with its inverse "sacrament" producing worldly bread and wine out of the divine grace of Christ's sacrifice, it also made an end to the Hildebrandian papacy as a unifying force in Latin Christendom. Having negotiated first the sacramental mediation between God and man (in the epoch of Berengar and Hildebrand, at B), and second the nature and institutionalization of the divine presence (in the epoch of Innocent III and the Fourth Lateran Council, at D) the obviation of the medieval core symbol now brought to issue, by making it problematic, the third term in the mediation: man.

Precisely because it had been so objectively and exclusively concerned with the divine in doctrine, ethos, and institution, the culture of the post-Boniface era rendered itself inadvertently contingent upon the human. It was no accident that it had been the economic exactions of secular rulers like Edward I of England and Philip the Fair upon the clergy that drove Boniface VIII to hyperbolic assertion of authority and to ecclesiastical capitalism. Secularism in the form of national monarchies and mercantile cities had become a potent force. The more intellectual expression of the contingency was a widespread and often diffuse movement known as humanism. Often counterposed directly to the scholasticism representing the legacy of Abelard's epoch, humanism surfaced in many forms, from the implicit subtleties of Chaucer and Boccaccio to the later, self-conscious criticism of Erasmus of Rotterdam. Perhaps the most familiar, and also the most idealistic, of these forms was the classical humanism of the Italian quattrocento, the Renaissance.

Because my concern here is with articulation and obviation of a cultural core symbol, however, rather than with the ebb and flow of Western history, I shall represent the medieval epoch of man through a clerical figure. John Wycliffe was a scholarly cleric who lived much of his life at Oxford, and was a political affiliate of John of Gaunt, duke of Lancaster. His influential writings, produced late in his life, constitute a powerful critique of what he called the "visible church," and were a source of inspiration to the Lollards in England and the Czech reformers and revolutionaries of Jan Hus. He also wrote on the eucharist, dealing specifically with Berengar's teachings, and here the criticisms of his opponents are most significant. They accused Wycliffe of having no clear position on the eucharist, whereas he, a skilled realist theologian, had in fact located his position outside the purview of scholastic theology.

As an Oxonian realist, Wycliffe had been concerned with the relationship of *accidentia* to *substantia,* and wondered how the *accidentia* of the bread and wine could persist after the transubstantiation of their *substantia* into the body of Christ. If *accidentia* could have a being without an essence (*substantia*), why bother about essence? In his book, *De Eucharistia* (1379), Wycliffe denied transubstantiation, arguing that the *substantia* of Christ's body remains in heaven in union with its *accidentia.* The effectiveness of the eucharist, then, lies in its effect on the mind and soul of the worshiper: its aim, according to Wycliffe, is to cause an "indwelling" of Christ in the soul.[9] Whatever the "actuality" or corporality of the sacramental elements, in other words, their real importance involves an effect on the worshiper, the "man" in the mediation.

In his philosophical denial of the separability of *accidentia* and *substantia,* Wycliffe had negated, for his epoch, the contribution of the scholastics of the "twelfth-century renaissance" to sacramental doctrine. In other writings, such as his *De potestate papae* (also 1379), papal authority and the organization of the "visible church" is attacked, thus indicting also the societization of the twelfth-century epoch.

The theology and criticism of Wycliffe represent the epoch of the final cancellation of the medieval cycle, at point *F* (fig. 18). The trope of divine presence and papal theocracy meets its resolution in Wycliffe's heretical insight: the divine, however corporeally embodied in the eucharist, remains resolutely divine (and in heaven); from the standpoint of man, the worshiper, a sign (such as, for instance, Berengar's symbol) is quite

9. Macdonald, *Berengar,* 409.

enough. As a realization of the divine presence, Wycliffe's "in-dwelling in Christ in the soul" combines the subtlety of Ber-engar with the flexibility of transubstantiation. It is, neverthe-less, still medieval in that the "center of gravity" remains with God. For the century that followed Wycliffe, described by Jan Huizinga as the "waning of the Middle Ages," the issue lay between the church, conciliar reform of the church, and out-spoken mysticism or denial of the church.

Divinity—God via his son, as a presence in the sacrament—

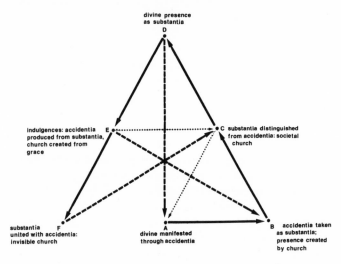

FIGURE 18: Cancellation of medieval cycle.

was the *substantia,* the essence or ground of being of the me-dieval era. *Accidentia,* the world of sensuous, outward appear-ance, produced as "visible church" through indulgences, de-duced by the Neoplatonism of twelfth-century scholastics, and adduced by Erigena as the figurative manifestation of God, moves as the retrograde implication and motivating resistance of the tropes that articulate *substantia.* Wycliffe's denial of their separation, one of the profoundest insights of medieval times, mediated the closure of the entire sequence.

The two manifestations of this closure—point *G,* the not-

not of the medieval sequence—have seldom been considered as dual implications of the same epoch. And yet the "age of scientific discovery," of Copernicus, Galileo, Columbus, and Magellan, and the outbreak of the Protestant Reformation, were two sides of the same coin. *Accidentia* was discovered as nature, not in Erigena's sense of the figurative manifestation of God, but as a new, secular ground of being, in the very epoch in which *substantia,* the presence of God, was determined by Luther and others to be a function of human faith. Thus the epoch of Reformation was the point at which Western culture, not having a stabilizing ritual, fell through its figure-ground reversal.

The Middle Ages had a significant if implicit notion of *natura,* shared with, and reinterpreted from, the writers of classical antiquity. It was also, arguably, the most technologically sophisticated civilization known up to that point. But, for all the subtlety of its weapons and windmills, water-powered forges and fulling mills, it did not generate a Copernican plurality of worlds or a Newtonion mystique of "direct action at a distance," because its ground of being was centered on a palpable trope, the "now" of divine presence. It was too centered, as an era, upon the epoch of salvation to spare energy and credibility for a decentered world of number and spatial plurality. Medieval civilization was a continual reform movement, motivated against the perceived secularization of its internal resistance— nature, society and reason, and production. Only after Wycliffe had articulated the union of *substantia* and *accidentia,* in what we might call the pre-Reformation era, did the first effective mechanical clocks appear in Europe.

The third closure of the medieval cycle, point *G,* coincides with the not-not of point *A,* and also, because it is the epoch of inversion, with point *A* of the modern cycle. In sacramental terms, the closure mediates between the notion of the worshiper's involvement in the acquiring of grace (as in the indulgences at point *E*) and Wycliffe's ideal of "an indwelling of Christ in the soul" and his contempt for the visible church. This was achieved in various ways in the Reformation by what we could call the "humanization" of *substantia* or divine presence (the concomitant of the naturalization of *accidentia* by scientists and explorers), and by the setting up of new churches or congregations in opposition to the Roman church. Luther's doctrine of consubstantiation carries an echo of Erigena's pantheism in its insistence on the omnipresence of Christ ("the right hand of God is everywhere"), but makes the *substantia* of the eucharist a sacramental union of the two substances—human and divine—of Christ. Thus Luther's not-not denies the purely figurative *(accidentia)* sacrament of Erigena by asserting a real divine presence, but confutes the dogma of transubstantiation by including a human, as well as a divine, *substantia* in the divine presence. Consubstantiation therefore includes the act of mediation within the eucharist, making it a microcosm of the man-God relation, rather than merely an element in the relation. Calvin's articulation of the not-not, receptionism, could be said to return to Erigena's concept of man as the *copula mundi,* the catalyst of the world. For Calvin, as for Wycliffe, Christ's body remains in heaven, but it can be received by the faithful in a mystical way, depending upon the condition (the faith) of the recipient.

Whatever their positions on the real presence (and Luther and Calvin can be said to have negotiated the not-not of Erigenian figurativism in opposite ways), both reformers, as well as the Lutheran and Reformed religions that followed them, made man's salvation a function of faith or conscience. And this meant that the collective point of orientation, God, became a relative revelation rather than an absolute mystery, for the faith upon which a knowledge of God was conditional depended upon a particular religious teaching, and hence upon a social body and tradition. Because man was responsible to God, the Reformation made him responsible for God. And if the covenant with God thus becomes a function of man's covenant with man, what is to stop it from revealing itself in its true colors as social contract, and what is to stop faith from becoming reason? This transformation is, in a sense, the essence of the Western figure-ground reversal.

This perspective change in common focus or responsibility—man taking responsibility for the conventional rather than trying to compel it as "mystery" through trope—corresponds to a formal shift in obviational encompassment. As a point of transition, the not-not turns itself from an internal, encompassed to an external, encompassing epoch, and it everts the nature-society-symbol (production) mediation in the process. Thus in the cycle of modernity, that of the bourgeoisie, hierarchy and trope become an "internal" resistance (become, in Dumont's word, "shamefaced"), whereas the "resistance" of the medieval cycle, egalitarian ratonality, becomes the major thrust and compulsion of cultural movement ("progress").

Accordingly, the epoch following the Reformation, that of the English Puritans and the religious wars, often styled the "reformation of the Reformation," belongs to the "internal" mediation of modernity. As point B, corresponding to the medieval epoch of Hildebrand and sacramental reform, it represents here an *internal* sacramental salvation, in terms of the Calvinist concept of predestination. It also achieved a remarkable expression in Cornelis Jansen's Calvinist Augustinianism (1640)—his severe doctrine of original sin and countervailing divine grace—and in the contemporary absolutist notion of the divine right of monarchs. The Puritan notion of the "elect" that spelled the downfall of Charles I merely exchanged one of these doctrines for another.

In terms of nature, this was the epoch in which Kepler formulated mathematically the hierarchy of planetary motions (1609, 1618), and Galileo (1634, in his "Dialogue on Two New Sciences . . .") framed the principles of motion and inertia, both of them germinal to Newton's later "divine clockwork" of direct action at a distance. But the philosophical basis of the transition from faith to reason was articulated by Descartes in his *Discourse on Method* (1637). Descartes spoke of two kinds of *substantia:* "thinking substance" or mind, and "extended substance," the spatial or material plurality of *accidentia* or nature. His famous duality restated the medieval scholastic opposition of essence and accident in the modern terms of mind and its (natural) object—society (or culture) and nature—and thus framed the conditions of the modern core symbol.

The epoch of the early to mid 1600s is more familiar for the

violence of its religious wars than for its remarkable and remarkably self-confident ambitions. It was the era of Oliver
Cromwell's lord protectorship and of the Fronde and the for-
tified Jansenist strongpoints in France. Taken in its own terms,
this "troubled period" before the accession of the Sun King
(which, nevertheless, gave the Sun King the inspiration and
rationale for his absolutism) is too radical to fit well into anyone's orderly account of the rise of Western institutions.

Like its medieval counterpart, the succeeding epoch, point
C, was that of society and the collective mode of thought,
reason. But whereas the (dialectical) reason of the medieval
scholastics served sacramental doctrine largely as a catalyst,
providing the terms of essence and accident, the modern era of
Enlightenment constituted a pivotal ideological realization. It
drew its basic conceptual orientation from Descartes (as its
precursor, Isaac Newton, drew his from Kepler and Galileo),
and substituted a publicly held and collectively articulated reason for the innate faith of predestination, and an innate natural
"clockwork" mechanism for the divine presence.

The Enlightenment, with its *Encyclopédie* and enlightened
despots, its *philosophes,* its journal-oriented "public" (they became "citizens" in the following era) and public-oriented jour-
nalists, constituted the modern discovery of collective enterprise. It was, perhaps, Luther's "conscience" made self-conscious and aware of itself as "reason," Descartes's "thinking
substance" focused on the "extended substance" of nature that
served the age as a ground of being.[10] Society, like reason, was
understood to be an artificial construct, a kind of sacramental
figure or induction of the rational order of nature. This was
most significantly articulated in Montesquieu's *The Spirit of
Laws* (1748) and in Rousseau's conclusive *Social Contract*
(1762). As nature was the (extended) plurality of divine epoch,
so society (and its reason) was the ordered plurality of human
artifice, understanding, and governance. Copernican cosmol-
ogy had generated its cultural and social counterpart.

10. "Science" is "conscience" without the "con."

As the "faith" or "conscience" that the Reformation, following Wycliffe, saw as the human function of divine will, became an innate "predestination" in Cromwell's time, so the rational society of the Enlightenment was subsequently internalized. Reason was a human "function" for the Enlightenment, a liberating principle, as conscience had been for Luther, but it was not yet a predestination or destiny. Writers such as Voltaire, Diderot, or Franklin as well as autocratic rulers—Frederick the Great, Maria Theresa and her son Joseph II, and Catherine the Great—could be apostles of the liberating power of reason. For the epoch that followed, however, reason became inevitable, like the "categorical imperative" of one of its philosophers, Immanuel Kant, or the triumphant march of the "world-historical spirit" of another, Hegel. Substitution D, supplanting a civil, philosophical "reason" with an internalized rational mandate, made enlightenment itself a despot.

It had its "elect," the bourgeoisie, whose interests and ideals triumphed in the American and French revolutions, and eventually became the mode of constitutional monarchy as well, and it had its wars, some of them approaching the earlier religious wars in scope and devastation. For the twentieth century, the emergence of rationalism as a political form was a kind of charter of democratic ideals; we should not forget, though, that democracy is the "numerical" and plural form of government, as finance is of economics, or science of knowledge. It should also not be forgotten that, in addition to Washington and Robespierre, Napoleon Bonaparte fought for the mandate of reason, and did so as tragically and fruitlessly as Cromwell had for *his* mandate.

The age that enthroned the goddess Reason, and that held, with Thomas Jefferson, the equality and the inalienable rights of man to be "self-evident," represents the sort of apotheosis of the modern cycle that the era of Innocent III and Aquinas did of the medieval. It was the time of Beethoven and Mozart, as well as Kant and Hegel, and it harbored a great critic in Goethe, who attempted to found a natural science centered on human meaning, and decried telescopes and microscopes as

magnifying the insignificant.[11] Perhaps the best evocation of
the epoch in its relation to Copernican plurality and moral
mandate was Kant's slogan of "the moral law within us and
the starry sky above us."

Reason and rational politics were an *ethos* for man, a mode
of mind (Descartes's "thinking substance") modeled on the
order and regularity of Newtonian nature (Descartes's "extended substance"). Rational order in the cosmos, the artifact
of Voltaire's "watchmaker God," was a kind of literal and mathematical equivalent of Erigena's world as figurative sacrament,
divine essence apprehended as conventional order rather than
holy mystery. And it was also the opposite of the "faith" and
"conscience" of the reformers, for, instead of rendering man
savable through a spark of revealed divine discernment, reason
rendered God tenable as the precedent of bourgeois conventional order—a bigger and better Isaac Newton contemplating
man's contemplation of His works from on high.

The rationalists of future epochs would not always be willing to extend their salvation to the divine in this way. But for
the moment, the epoch in which conscience had become rational culture, God existed as the Supreme Artificer or as the
utterly mystical godhead of Swedenborg, Blake, and Beethoven's *Heiliger Dankgesang*. In terms of obviation, this epoch,
point *D,* marks the first cancellation of the accomplished modern trope (fig. 19). The divine presence had become wholly
artifact, *accidentia* as against the *substantia* of the High Gothic,
and the intellectual salvation of God instead of the spiritual
salvation of man. Luther's consubstantiation and Calvin's receptionism enacted a religious and sacramental *sharing* of figure
and ground for an age in which figure and ground had become
dubious and confused (and Luther had also voiced his opposition to the decentered Copernican model). But the epoch of
bourgeois revolution made God, as a function of nature, a practical ubiquity but a spiritual specter, rather like the theme of a
string quartet.

---

11. His great *Faust* in this regard is almost a satire.

The medieval epoch of production or symbol, at point *E,* represented a desperate attempt on the part of the "papal monarchy," and something of an undercurrent in medieval life. But its modern equivalent and obviational inverse witnessed the conclusive articulation of the Western core symbol, and the accession of Western (imperialist) civilization to world domination. Although the modern epoch constituted the most rapid

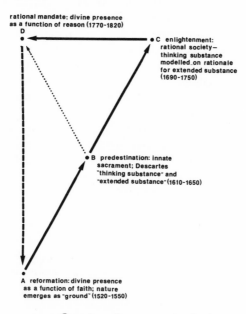

FIGURE 19: Conscience becomes rational culture.

and radical technological transformation in recorded history, its motivation was not so much technological as symbolic. Reason was no longer Lutheran conscience become self-conscious, a philosophy applied to ethical existence, or even a political mandate; as culture, law, means of production, it engaged the natural ground of being in a thoroughly dynamic transformative relation.

The symbolic statement of this relation is the symbology

that David M. Schneider has found to infuse American family and kin relations,[12] and to organize and motivate American culture generally in all of its aspects as a "core" or "epitomizing" symbol.[13] "Blood" kinship, an educated person, or a modern automobile or jet aircraft (*and* the process of its operation) all exemplify, in the conceptualization of the "natives" themselves, the productive interrelation of culture and nature. In the epoch of its invention, this dynamic was attributed to nature, in Darwin's *Origin of Species* (nature as evolution—the productive process of order rather than the artifact of a "watchmaker" God), as well as to culture, in the writings of Marx and Engels (culture as man's production of himself). Both the financial capitalism of the imperialist-industrial age and the concomitant labor movement and socialism trace their roots to the symbolic dynamic of production.

Both terms of the relation were suffused by the dynamic and were recast in its image. By the end of the epoch, the basic terms of nature (space, time, and inertia, in Einstein's relativity theory) and those of culture (language, personality, and worldview, in the cultural relativity of Franz Boas) were understood to be relative—functions of the viewpoint of the observer, or of the subjects themselves. Thus the Cartesian distinction between "thinking substance" and "extended substance," at point *B,* was cancelled by a conception of thought and extension as relative coproducts of one another, just as the "innate sacrament" of the Calvinists was countered by the overt, productive sacrament of nature and culture.

As the inevitable (re-)integration of Copernican-Newtonian natural plurality with bourgeois social and cultural plurality, production and its epoch (from about 1860 to the first decade of the twentieth century) mark the realization of the modern trope of quantity and spatiality. Production and quantity became ends in themselves, fostering the plurality of mass pro-

12. David M. Schneider, *American Kinship* (Chicago: University of Chicago Press, 1980).

13. David M. Schneider, "Notes toward a Theory of Culture," in K. Basso and H. Selby, eds., *Meaning in Antropology* (Albuquerque: University of New Mexico Press, 1976).

duction, and ultimately, "the masses," humanity as pluralism alone. Neither rational nature nor rational society was in itself tenable or viable following the trope of their dynamic combination. Nietzsche, a witness to the process, and an astute critic, wrote of the "transvaluation of all values," and Marx, who saw firsthand the widespread removal of production from the family context, spoke with invective of the alienation of the worker from the fruits of his labor.

In a somewhat broader sense, perhaps, than he intended for it, Marx's comment on the modern "sacrament" of production echoes Wycliffe's criticism of transubstantion: What does the eucharist profit the worshiper if he is not included in its transformation? Expanding a bit on Marx, we can paraphrase: What happens to the *meaning* of the productive act—the dynamic integration of nature and culture—when it is immediately transformed into the mere plurality of money? Does not the product itself supplant the meaning of its production and, especially in mechanized or mass production, automatically substitute quantity (or convenience, or teleology) for meaning? Does not production, whose epoch led to the relativization of culture as well as nature, amount to the liquidation of meaning, *counting* it out of existence through object fetishism and plurality?

As for Wycliffe, it all comes down to the human element, as a point of contingency, whose participation (salvation) has been preempted by an all-too-effective cultural trope. The epoch succeeding that of production is one that, as in the medieval era of John Wycliffe in the 1300s, make the person—man, and human participation in meaningful articulation—central to its concern. This is the present epoch, point F in the modern cycle, which took form during the world wars, and emerged in the mid to late twentieth century. It can be identified with existentialism and phenomenology, and with that obsessive concern with self that Richard Sennett has analyzed as modern narcissism. As an (internal) closure, it synthesizes the opposition between the mandate of reason (D: self-evident human rights) and production (E: productive assimilation of nature and reason): production is treated as internal and self-evident, and valued in terms of extraneous and human-centered meanings. This is the age of consumerism, the technological (including *chemical*) production of the individual through the special properties of machines, drugs, and ultimately the computer. It is also the era of the synthesis of human needs and meanings through the media—advertising, entertainment, and the "news."

The reflexive use of collective techniques and organization to produce the individual brings this epoch into a negative

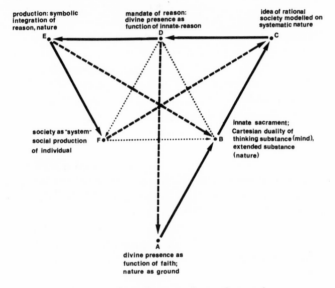

FIGURE 20: Cancellation in the modern cycle.

opposition to that of the Enlightenment *(C)*, for the Enlightenment was concerned to produce a collective order or organization through the application of individual human reason. Thus the mode of cancellation here (the final one of the modern cycle, fig. 20) is that of the one as against the many, the trope (which is here the means of advertising, phenomenology, and contemporary literary studies) versus the representational symbol. Society, the ideal and the goal of the Enlightenment,

is internalized and taken for granted here as is production—
it is "the system" or "the establishment." As an "internal"
critique of the modern trope, and the mediative point in the
trope's coming to grips with its own not-not, our contemporary
epoch realizes the third and final cancellation of the modern
cycle.

Intriguing as it might be to speculate on the character of a
modern not-not at a future point G, it is beyond the scope of
this study. A trope is elicited, not determined, and thus it is not
predictable. To reiterate a most important point: I am concerned here with the temporal development of the Western core
symbol as a process of tropic expansion and obviation, and not
with the course of history itself. A doctrinal skeleton, such as
is presented here, will do very nicely, though most of what is
fascinating and important in history—Shakespeare, the Eliza-
bethan era, the Romantic period, the rise of cities—is left out.
Likewise, although the form of obviation is inevitably cyclical,
this does not necessarily imply that history or culture is cyclical
in the way that some writers have portrayed it.

The medieval and modern core symbols have developed in
relation to each other through a holographic process of figure-
ground reversal. Thus the medieval core symbol of the eucharist was articulated in a cumulative effort of reform against the
"secularizing" tendencies of an internal opposite. To illustrate:
the literalization of the sacrament in the Hildebrandian reform
was asserted in anticipation of the rationalism that was to compromise Abelard, and was already manifest in the School of
Chartres, and its product, Berengar. The efforts of Bernard of
Clairvaux, the Carthusians, and others to free monastic society
of secularizing influences, and the separation of *substantia* from
accidentia in the doctrine of transubstantiation, were effected
against the "resistance" of a worldliness that became church
policy under Boniface VIII, but was already underway by the
time of the Crusades (when [nonmonetary] papal "indulgence"
was granted to crusaders). Finally, John Wycliffe's attacks on
the "visible church" and its miraculous transformation of
worldly into divine substance defended a vision of a purified

religion not only against the politicized papal system of his day, but also against the retrograde implication from the Reformation (already evident in cultic movements of his day) of immediately accessible grace.

The mediation of nature, society (reason), and production that the medieval sequence produced dialectically within itself comprises the collective or conventional side of the dialectic. This is, of course, the side that is obviated in the articulation of the medieval trope, which is hierarchical and differentiating. When the consubstantiation and receptionism of the Reformation substituted a collective and conventional "figure" (and, perforce, an individuating "ground"), the "sides" of the obviation also shifted. The "conventional" points, A, C, and E, became external, and the "differentiating" apices of the medieval trope, B, D, and F, became internal and obviated. The shift in perspective entailed in this figure-ground reversal can be seen in figure 21, where the "conventional" points A, C, and E can either form the internal mediation of a (foreground, upright) triangle or the external, encompassing mediation of a (background, inverted) triangle.

The medieval trope was an expression of continual and cumulative reform and refinement of received scriptural revelation, against the resistance of an internally generated collectivism. In a sense, medieval religiosity motivated its own differentiation to the point where Wycliffe, denying papacy, church, and transubstantiation, must perforce locate its instrument as well as its object in an ethereal and purely contemplative realm. It was not only an invisible, but an impossible, church. The modern trope, by contrast, had put its reform, in the Reformation, behind it; it was motivated by a compulsion of forward-directed implication (like the compulsion of the *habu*) rather than a resistance. In its own terms, this compulsion has been expressed variously as "man's self-perfection through Reason," the march of Hegel's "world-historical spirit," "progress," or simply "culture." The best analytic example is Weber's account of the Protestant ethic and its transformation into the spirit of capitalism. The Calvinists' notion of predestination was not medieval, but part of the internal, dialectically produced hierarchicism of the modern sequence. Its implication surfaces again in the triumphant bourgeois enthronement of Reason as divine in epoch *D,* and also in the north-European pietism of that period. The third term of the internal mediation is evident in the hypertrophied individuation (narcissism) and professionalism of our contemporary epoch.

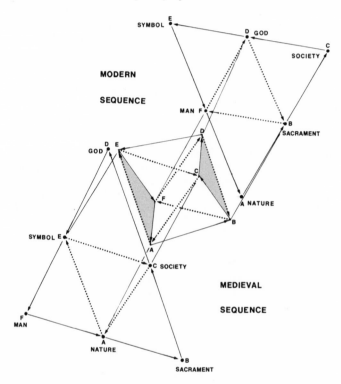

FIGURE 21: The medieval-modern reversal.

The medieval and modern tropes each replicated the other as an internal, motivating factor because, basically, each trope is formed against the other. This is the significance of the figure-ground reversal. Taken as a whole, the meaning of this double trope is involute: it generates its own referential space, stands for itself, and is about itself. The perceptions that make

one or the other facet distinct—the singular world of transcendental divine presence, or the plural world of production
and Copernican space—are folded into each other in the figure-
ground reversal.

These self-contained characteristics are part of the model,
and of the modeled core symbol in the form of its expansion.
They are not necessarily attributable to the course of Western
history apart from this, nor to the institutions and personalities
participating in it. History itself is knowable only through simplification, and its "happening" interacts with an immense
range of internal and external factors, cultural and noncultural,
human and nonhuman. The Roman church and the papacy, for
example, remained as a powerful force in modern life (especially in the period of Counter-Reformation and that of the
Bourbon and Hapsburg absolutism that followed) long after
its role as the prime unifier of Latin Christendom had been
obviated.

What the model articulates is the mythic component of history, a "simplification," from the viewpoint of conventional
time, in which time becomes "transparent" and cyclicality becomes that of resolvable epoch rather than a plural and spatial
repetition. The meaningful component of history is capable of
being resolved just precisely because it has been separated out
as a "Platonic" generic, because it eschews the practical and
normative issues of how meaning is linked to social action, and
the ideal issues of what is truth and what sort of justice ought
to prevail.

To be confronted with one's meaningful frame of reference
in unfamiliar form—to be told, for instance, that the strain of
rationalist, scientific skepticism from Descartes to the modern
era is the critical facade of an unexamined commitment to plurality and number—is, perhaps, discomfiting. But it is a better
sort of objectivity than the unthinking acceptance of major
propositions so that one can be clinically precise about minor
ones.

If the analysis of the Daribi core symbol through obviation
made time problematic, and the discussion of time brought the

Western core symbol, and its figure-ground reversal, to issue, then this analysis of the latter brings us back to the heuristic of this study itself. What is the significance of figure-ground reversal, as I have used it, in relation to symbolic point of reference and to the embodied meaning of obviation?

7 Conclusion: Third-order Trope and the Human Condition

The focus and central point of this discussion is that a single phenomenon or principle *constitutes* human culture and cultural capability. I have called this phenomenon "trope" for its most familiar manifestation as the perception of meaning within cultural reference points. The phenomenon is coherent and pervasive, organizing conditions for the perception of meaning over the whole scale-range of cultural forms. But wherever it appears, it is the same phenomenon; *it is holographic throughout the range.* The expansion of trope from point metaphor to cultural frame, and the higher "powers" or orders of trope, represent merely the same principle, applied, continuously or discontinuously, to progressively higher orders of containment. Thus trope has no structure, system, or mechanism; what appears as complexity in an obviation diagram is merely the effect of its recursive implications on cultural convention. As holistic perception, trope is always *epoch,* the "now" or presence of time, as discussed in chapter 5, and as such is always capable of being analyzed or depicted synchronically.

The *orders* of trope can be said to constitute or organize the large-scale parameters of cultural symbolism. They might better be described as "powers" in the mathematical sense, as each is formed as *the trope of* the preceding order. Thus second-order trope, or figure-ground reversal, encountered in the discussions of the Daribi and Western core symbols, is the trope of the perception constituted by first-order trope. Third-order trope, whose implications will be explored presently, is formed as the trope of reversibility. (Note that this cannot amount simply to the reversal of a reversal, for that would merely reapply the second power.) Before considering the wider implications of the powers of trope, let me categorize each briefly:

First-order trope; the elicitation of meaning as a perception in symbolic value space, as part of a cultural dialectic of referentiality (microcosm) and image (macrocosm).

Second-order trope; the trope of perception, figure-ground reversal. The principle of orientational relativity and reversibility within the cultural dialectic, enabling reference points (names) to be treated as images and vice versa.

Third-order trope; the trope of reversibility, embodiment. Folds figure-ground reversal around itself to constitute bodily microcosm and macrocosm respectively as bounding parameters of the human condition.

It should be clear that, although the powers appear at first to form a hierarchical succession, their order is in fact recursive, as third-order trope constitutes the parameters (microcosmic/macrocosmic) between which first-order trope mediates. Furthermore, since third-order trope accomplishes this by setting up the *body* as a macrocosm in relation to the "mental" microcosm of the cultural dialectic, the relation *between* first- and third-order tropes is the same as that within the dialectic. Their relationship is holographic.

The role of the second power, figure-ground reversal, is consistent with this. As the enabler of reversibility, it permits the interchangeability of symbolic reference point and image in the dialectic of trope expansion, and it also serves as the medial and facilitating term between embodied microcosm ("mind") and embodying macrocosm ("body"). Second-order trope is part of the holographic relation.

The holographic consistency that exists within the epoch of tropic expansion, and among the powers of trope, manifests the unity of the constitutive phenomenon. But the *distribution* of the powers over several orders of encompassment corresponds to another crucial fact of cultural constitution: that the total range of issues involved in meaning cannot be resolved at one "level" or locus, or within one dialectic. This is why issues such as those of culture, relativity, the individual and society, and meaning itself remain persistent ones for anthropology.

To an important degree these issues come together holographically, and for the same reason that the powers of trope do—because they are parts of a larger human phenomenon and are not "independent" problems. Since this final chapter concerns the expansion of trope from its second to its third power, I shall consider the issues topically as a part of that discussion, beginning with the problem of "culture." First, however, let me clarify the distributive necessity of the "issues."

It comes down, once again, to the definition of meaning. The sign, for Saussure, was a point of mediation between concept and percept, whereas meaning, for this study, is elicited as an image or perception between cultural reference points. A sign can be defined precisely, and can be assigned discrete functions in an exact science of semiotics; a trope can be elicited but not defined, and it can only *approach* the extremes of referentiality or complete self-containment as boundary conditions. Thus, for obviation, the collective and the individuative are *relative* approximations that can never attain the precision of semiotic sign or function because they cannot be defined that closely. Their relative nature is a consequence of second-order trope, in its enabling of the dialectic through reversibility.

But then, of course, an absolute realization of collectivity or individuation—of referentiality or iconicity—is impossible within the microcosm of meaning, which, as a mediative process, can only *represent* its bounding and defining parameters. Individuality can only be constituted in a relative sense (as "representation," in Schopenhauer's terms) *within* the mind, because it is constituted in an absolute sense *as* the mind. Collectivity can only be constituted relatively within the mind because it is actually realized *among* minds. The third power of trope, embodying macrocosm as against embodied microcosm, is thus a crucial ingredient of meaning.

Perception, hence meaning, can only take place within the individual mind. Perhaps this is what Edward Sapir meant when he said that culture can only be constituted within the individual. But in order to perceive, the mind must be able to perceive the self *as* a body. This is so not only because the body is the *phenomenon* of the mind, the "other side" of the brain's neuronic connections, but also because the perception of self as *body* is necessary to its orientation ("in space") as a perceiver. In order to perceive *culturally,* according to conventional reference points, the perceptive faculty requires consociation—the tutelage of language, and of a plurality of minds. Just as materialism often forgets that we have minds, so structuralism and semiotics, with their absolute definitions of meaning functions, can be fairly accused of forgetting that we have bodies.

What, then, of the implications of this coherent organizing concept, trope, for our understanding of culture and the human condition? The argument that the basic frames of culture are formed as large-scale tropes, essentially like myths, implies that cultural meanings live in a constant flux of continual re-creation. It also implies that the core of culture is not a haphazard assemblage of customs, ideas, objects, institutions, words, and the like, but a coherent flow of images and analogies, that cannot be communicated directly from mind to mind, but only elicited, adumbrated, depicted. It is constituted not of the signs of conventional reference, nor of the individual's private percepts of "things in the world," but within a reversible dialectic that moves *between* these limits. This makes possible the phenomena of collectively elicited trope as well as of the embedding of conventional reference within the private worlds of individual perception.

The sense of "invention," and the certainty that human beings have what Leonardo Da Vinci, following Aristotle, spoke of as "internal sense faculties,"[1] the perception *within* the mind that I have equated with meaning, has been all but lost in the emphasis of scientific empiricism on external sense faculties alone. Modern neuropsychology knows the "internal" faculties as the "spatial" sensitivities of the "right" neocortical hemisphere, and modern writers on aesthetics and Gestalt psychology could scarcely fail to take them into account. Before these faculties were put by in deference to the sign-world of

1. David Summers, *The Judgement of Sense: Studies in the Language of Renaissance Art* (Cambridge University Press, 1986).

rationalism and materialism, Renaissance and early modern thinkers attempted many times to make them the basis of an education through the directly sensible, concrete image. The effort to educate the concrete, as against the abstract, imagination underlies our conception of museums, and Shakespeare's Globe Theatre (and his idea of drama and its effect) was based on it. The notion of internal faculties played a role in Leibniz's formulation of the monads, and Goethe tried to make "the exact, concrete imagination" the basis of a radical natural science, founded on meaning rather than abstraction.

For anthropology, the problem has been that of articulating this potential, and the world of conceptualization and operation that it implies, with a natural science format. This means largely that invention and the concrete imagination have had to be mystified or relegated to the realm of "intuition" and placed in a defensive posture. The fullest explication—in what are often described as "mystical" terms—of culture in this sense has been that of Oswald Spengler, and its most familiar expression in American anthropology is the "configurationalism" of Ruth Benedict (though other configurationalists, including Bateson, Mead, Kroeber, and perhaps even Boas, were sensitive to it). Perhaps the status of anthropology at that time, struggling for recognition as a "science," and perhaps the "translation" of this idea through the writings of Benedict, Kroeber, and Spengler, was at fault, but in any case none of those who sought to formulate its premises anthropologically were able to bring it to the point of direct conceptual contrast with the empiricism of a sign-based scientific outlook. Perhaps, again, the notion of "internal faculties" was just too much of a thing unto itself, and had to be "patched in" to the science of culture according to the specific formulations of whoever chose to do so.

At any rate, the attempt to introduce Spenglerian cultural cycles or Benedictian "patterns" as scientific phenomena without explicating their internal dynamic—what makes them patterned or cyclical—is to mystify them and beg the intuitive faculty. Spengler, in *The Decline of the West*, based his effort explicitly on Goethe's approach to the natural sciences, and on what he called Nietzsche's "overview," but again, given his position as a European scholar, this was an invocation of cultural resources that had only a tangential address to the scientific. In the meantime, the issue of culture's internal dynamic had been broached, and subverted, via the rationality and emphasis on *external* faculties stressed by the empiricism of ethnosemantics, and the Saussurian positivism of Lévi-Strauss. The French master was by no means insensitive to Spengler, and his work—particularly in *The Savage Mind* and the *Mythologiques* series—has had a very positive and educative effect in reorienting anthropology to the study of meaning. But structuralism, for all of its creative and sensitive exploration, for instance, of the workings of myth, remains resolutely committed to the Saussurian formulation of sign and meaning, and results in an abstract, rather than a concrete, explication of cultural imagery.

Structuralism, by emphasizing the found intangibles of abstract category, renders trope and its imagery tangential—lost tangibles that surface only in the operations performed upon armatures and matrices. Image blends interchangeably with the iconic expressions found on the artist's canvas, in the silver nitrate of photographic emulsion, or upon the "internal retinas" of the brain. Practiced and learned as a part of learning culture, the facility to form images in this way is also that of responding to the elicitation of reference points; employed on an expanded scale it "reads" meaning in the extension of conventional "point" trope into larger cultural frames. The effect of such a "reading" is to cancel, in a sequential and cumulative fashion, the abstract points of reference, via the formation of progressively more inclusive and encompassing images, until the point of obviation—the self-encompassing of the frame itself—is reached. Thus obviation is the opposite of structuralism, for it makes the referential categories of convention peripheral to its ultimate realization of an encompassing image. "Structure" is not singled out as the determinant of meaning, but rather *subsumed,* as orienting features of a landscape might be, within the coordinating binocular perspective that organizes detail into significance.

The actual "concreteness" of things are not qualities we can know collectively; to understand whether my "green" is the same as yours, or my personally formed image of the Mona Lisa, or experience of the *Eroica* Symphony, would indeed require some sort of intuition, or perhaps telepathy. We simply communicate (and learn) by exchanging conventional words, phrases, gestures, pictorial forms, work toward an effective refinement of their collective sense, and hope for the best. The perception of image is personal, and relative to the person.

We move, then, from one sin of which Spengler and the configurationalists were accused, intuition, to another—that of relativity. Lacking a generic—a means by which the intransigence of cultural image might be penetrated—the configurationalists considered it a matter of impressionistic quality alone, uniquely self-relative and permeable only to the intuition. (Equating the symbolic with its particularistic *content,* they individuated it to the point of uniqueness; Jung made the same equation, but collectivized instead.) Thus the definitive theoretical expression of cultural relativity came to be framed in extreme terms. If we supply a generic, however, approaching the core symbology of a culture via the expansion of trope, then this extreme statement of relativity is mitigated somewhat. Conventional coordinate systems and their differences are merely the surface phenomenon.

Cultural relativity, the self-evident intransigence of independent "coordinate systems," is only significant, it could be argued, insofar as it impinges upon, and implies, relativity *within* such a system. Relativity, the self-consciousness of meaning, is dangerous enough to be important only insofar as it places one's own meanings and the relations upon which they are based at hazard. The real peril posed by the exotic is not that of self-estrangement, but the possibility of a relativizing self-knowledge that such estrangement implies.

Relativity occurs when the flow of analogy is compromised by its own enabling condition of reversibility—when the expansion of first-order trope reaches its limit in second-order trope. This is *internal* relativity, and its ultimate locus is the individual perceiver, in resonance with the collective imagery of a culture at large. In times of uncertainty and ambivalent values, the public resonance of its implications evokes the very real danger of existential crisis.

In this regard Shakespeare's *Hamlet,* written less than a century after the cataclysmic events of the Reformation, was very much the "problem play" of its times. Prince Hamlet was a student at Luther's Wittenberg, and moves in a conscience-centered ethical world where there is neither good nor bad "but thinking makes it so." If his "tragic flaw" were merely an inability to act decisively, then the play would be a social pathology rather than a tragedy. It *is* a tragedy because it dramatizes a struggle to reach a conclusion on highly relativized ground. It was not that the Prince could not bring himself to act, but that he knew, and saw, too much.

Was "madness"—Hamlet's feigned insanity, Lear's *anomie* on the heath—Shakespeare's motif for the enactment of arbitrariness discovered at the very core of things? Are not the "fools" in all of the plays, with their repartee of disjointed scholastic logic, the foils of a profound internal culture shock? And if this is so, is not anthropology, with its well-known proclivity for the Bongo-Bongo, the foil of a modern internal relativity? We *deflect* a perceived internal relativity of values onto the conspicuous frontiers and interfacings of *cultural* value systems because (and here Fabian's thesis[2] comes to the fore) "the time is out of joint." Perhaps it made good political sense for Shakespeare to set his scenarios in other times and places, but if Sennett[3] is correct regarding the failure of Western social symbolism, the anthropologist *needs* concrete and indisputable[4] symbolic forms to objectify the theory and practice of issues that our own value crisis renders all too ambiguous.

2. Johannes Fabian, *Time and the Other: How Anthropology Makes Its Object* (New York: Columbia University Press, 1983).

3. Richard Sennett, *The Fall of Public Man* (New York: Alfred A. Knopf, 1977).

4. The "distancing" of "the field," spatially as well as methodologically, provides the strongest arguments for this indisputability. Given that his *experience* constitutes the real data, the anthropologist exercises the privilege of selecting among an indefinite range of equally valid "glosses" of its imagery as "explanation."

By constituting the cultural dialectic as a representational microcosm, the reversibility of second-order trope renders all of its meanings ultimately relative. Only the microcosm itself, the wholeness of the perceiver (and the holism of *epoch,* the act of perceiving), can be regarded as complete. But the microcosm, paradoxically, can only *perceive* itself as an individual through the recognition of other microcosms, of a collectivity. Thus it enters into another dialectic, the macrocosmic, or embodied dialectic of individual and society, encompassing the expansion of reversibility to its limit in third-order trope. Although the unity of trope as a phenomenon is intended epochally ("synchronically"), I shall make use of evidence relating to evolution and the brain in explicating this expansion.

A reversible field allows me to treat the cultural dialectic as being "everted" in the movement toward embodiment. Of course, it probably makes more sense from an evolutionary standpoint to speak of the dialectic as an "inversion" of its macrocosmic counterpart. In any case, "inside" and "outside" mark the "direction" or dimension of the macrocosmic expansion of the dialectic, and it is not difficult to imagine a selective pressure being applied simultaneously to brain and society. I shall begin with a fairly straightforward question: Why is the human brain, particularly the neocortex, so relatively large?

Like most simple questions, this one has a conventional, pat answer. And like most conventional, pat answers, it begs the question. This is that the brain is large because it has been specialized to allow human beings to encode and deal with a great deal of complexity. The possibilities of the brain in this respect are, indeed, prodigious, but the answer begs the question because complexity "in the world" is a function of the human brain itself, and complexity is by and large something that *we* have defined and projected onto things. A deer inhabits the same world, but the deer's world is seemingly less complex than ours, especially—since it does not contain mathematics or *The Rime of the Ancient Mariner*—in terms of *our* complexity.

Nor does it help to substitute "ecological niche" for "world" in this connection, for it turns out that such a niche is defined and enabled by the capabilities of the being that exploits it. Browsing up to a certain limit enables the deer's niche in part, projecting "complexity" upon the world enables ours, and an explanation based on evolving up to the complexity of one's niche begs the question again, suggesting that the brain is large because it is large.

In the development of brain "laterality"—the specialization of neocortical functions that seems to be unique to human beings—the coding and articulation of complexity tends to be associated with one[5] (normatively the "left") hemispheric specialty. The other specialty, that of the cyclopean perception of meaning as holistic and holographic, is associated with the other (normatively the "right"). Each specialty serves as a point of departure for the other; holistic perception without reference points is as useless and anomic as the coding and referencing of a meaningless world. There is evidence that the specialization and localization of these operations develops in the brain after birth, particularly after a child learns to speak, and that it is only from this time that the corpus callosum, which coordinates the two, begins to function.[6]

The neocortex, where these definitively human operations come into being, is of course only part of the total brain. It is contexted with the paleocortex, or midbrain, associated with homeostatic (trophotropic) functions,[7] and the brainstem, identified with the regulation of behavior and movement, in MacLean's model of the triune brain.[8] Each of these divisions stands necessarily in a relation of mutual interdependence with the others. But the neocortex deserves our special attention,

5. By "laterality" I mean primarily the separation of the functions, rather than their identification with one "side" or the other.

6. Howard Gardner, *The Shattered Mind* (New York: Vintage Press, 1975), 386.

7. Victor W. Turner, "Body, Brain, and Culture," *Zygon* 18, no. 3 (September 1983): 221–45.

8. Paul D. MacLean, "A Triune Concept of the Brain and Behavior," in *The Hinks Memorial Lectures,* ed. T. Boag and D. Campbell (Toronto: University of Toronto Press, 1973).

for in lateralization it incorporates two interdependent, but dialectically opposed, operations within the same basic structural division of the brain. This can be seen in the fact that lateralization is seldom, if ever, total—that each side of the brain can replicate, to some degree, the specializations of the other.[9]

Given that the neocortex shares the general bilateral symmetry of the overall mammalian form, this would indicate that symmetry has been redeployed in man so as to yoke the complementary functions into a single, coordinate unit. An analogy could be drawn with the pairing of opposed muscles in the limbs of higher animals, so that language and internal perception constitute between them a leverage, as it were, of mind.

Very well, then, why is this *comprehensile* (comprehending and prehensile) organ so large? The argument that I shall advance is that extreme development of the neocortex transformed the brain from a largely regulatory organ to an *organ of perception*. Its relative size can be understood on an analogy with the sensing organs of other creatures that live by perceptual acuity: the eyes of the raptors, the ears of the deer, the nose of the wolf.

But unless it is understood in the light of a very special condition, this argument is apt, for all the unity of the brain, to favor the "right" hemisphere. The condition is that of *embodiment,* and the necesssity it poses for my argument is that perception must be a matter of total life-condition if it is to ground the human adaptation. The mind must produce and elicit, as well as receive, perceptions; the perceptions must address and coordinate a world that is common to all perceivers; the coordinates must be largely the same for external and internal perceptions.

The embodiment of thought as language, primarily through the medium of sound, but also involving visual image and bodily gesture, satisfies all of these requirements. Language

9. The "normative" lateralization can be inverted, or it can be diffused through a low degree of specialization, both conditions identifiable with forms of left-handedness. It would seem possible that mutual hemispheric replicability is an enabling factor for human culture.

allows meaning to be projected and resonated outside of the mental microcosm via sensuous means. It establishes, moreover, a single referential standard for projected and internally performed perceptions. Thus the perceptive faculty, the "right" brain, has not only an augmented internal inventory within which to expand its holistic syntheses, but also an external world, a collectivity, a society of meaning projectors.

But the neocortex is not, in any case, a self-contained entity. It is part of a much more complicated brain, and is integrally related through all manner of balancing subordinate and superordinate functions of its other parts. Thus contexted, within the interplay of ergotrophic and trophotropic systems, the neocortical balance—the expansion of the hemispheres in adjustment to each other—becomes a relative and controlled, rather than a runaway, process. Beyond this, the brain is contexted within the body, and is itself made contingent and relative.

But then, of course, no organism is ever a self-contained entity either, and the contextual argument cuts both ways. For its very being, knowing, and life processes, the organism is contained within society and culture, and they, in turn, are organized, orchestrated, and activated through language in its intrinsic connection with meaning. Thus the body, which grounds the brain and its tensions, is in turn grounded by them: thought embodied as language is the figure-ground reversal of the brain, the means by which the microcosm slips out of itself to synthesize collective meaning.

Laterality is as much culture "inside" as culture is laterality "outside." The core of the phenomenon is neither of these, and is neither "determined" from the outside nor "hard-wired" on the inside: it is the figure-ground reversal that is both at once, and that constitutes the human adaptive niche simultaneously within human beings and among them.

The brain is not, of course, the "mind." It is, instead, the shape that the body gives to mind's microcosm: embodied microcosm within a larger macrocosm. What, then, of the embodiment of body, the macrocosm, as it expands into the dimension of "the one and the many"? The counterpart of the brain's synthesis of collective cultural image through language is the body's reproductive synthesis of another body. As the brain contains the microcosm of the mind within the macrocosm of the body, so the loins—in particular the uterus—contain the macrocosm of the body, as fetus, within a reproductive microcosm.

This, too, is accomplished through a figure-ground reversal. Here, however, instead of an internal, contained bilaterality that slips outside to contain itself, the reversal involves two external *kinds of bodies,* male and female, the slip *inward* to contain *another.*[10] Physically, and in the most obvious morphological terms, the genital organs of female and male are respectively involute and evolute versions of one another, an inversion that becomes the means, in coitus, of a single embodiment of the sexes. Conception and childbirth also share this inversion of direction, and may both be (the former in the happiest cases, the latter always) accompanied by uterine spasms.

But the reproductive acts, even in their gendered "embodiment" in the correlate sexual versions of the human image, cannot be treated apart from their cultural and social circumstances. Hence reproduction accomplishes the embodiment or imaging of the human form, from the "ground" of social and cultural relationship. It constitutes, physically, the individual out of the generic, as the neocortex constitutes, through language, the generic of collective image out of the individual.

Language has its counterpart, as a kind of productive tension that infuses the human condition, in the tonus of continual sexual attraction ("receptivity") that is equally distinctive of that condition. This is the social sexuality that forms the ground for the reproductive embodiment of offspring. Its features, not unsurprisingly, are also imaged within the human body, in the so-called epigamic traits, or secondary sexual characteristics, of lissome female form, broad hips, protuberant buttocks and breasts, and male stature, facial hair, broad shoulders, graying temples, deep voice, and so forth. Some recent speculation has

10. Understood as coordinate parties to the act of coitus, rather than as individuals, the male and female contain the transmission of semen within their loins and the movements of their loins.

linked this condition to upright posture and provisioning behavior.[11]

The embodied thought of language, and the sexuality of macrocosmic embodiment, the figure-ground reversals, respectively, of brain and body, are the extensional means by which we transcend our corporeal and mortal limitations. Only embodiment can overcome the solipsism of an entirely private perceptual faculty, so that thought is estranged from itself and rendered self-conscious through speech, body is estranged in engendering another body through another body, and through the elaborate "foreplay" of social sexuality. Thus a sociocultural "field" of "the one and the many" comes into being, one that is simultaneously a perceptual awareness of self and other.

A realm of dialectical possibilities—inside and outside—is not, however, sufficient for the constitution of an individual, or a species. The thought, the possibility, requires the deed. Microcosm holds it place through the arbitrage of fixed "reference points" of conventional language and culture. What, then, is the correlate *embodied* reference, the act or deed by which the human condition is established in the world? If microcosm is held in place by an invisible collective, macrocosm is established by a concrete fact of individuation.

This "fact," the completion of third-order trope, is also the necessary fourth figure-ground reversal that completes the folding of the cultural dialectic "around itself." It amounts to the reversal of the head and loins, at the one point in the life of every[12] individual when the human head is passed through the loins: that of parturition, or childbirth. (The fact that the head belongs to one individual, and the loins belong to another is neither disqualifying nor trivial, since it is the means by which "head" becomes "figure" to the "ground" of the loins, and one individual emerges from another.)

Parturition constitutes the individual, in the most final and

11. A concise but convincing case is made by C. Owen Lovejoy in his essay "The Natural Detective," *Natural History* 93, no. 10 (October 1984):24–28.

12. The exception, of course, is caesarian birth, but as an ontogenetic exception it proves, as we shall see, the phylogenetic rule.

concrete terms. But in the more general sense of trope as an epochal and acausal ring of possibilities, a *generic,* it constitutes the species as well. For the figure-ground reversal of head and loins clinches the expansion into macrocosm, one of whose implications is increasing brain size, whereas another, social sexuality, has been correlated with upright posture. It has been conjectured, and convincingly argued, for some time that increasing brain and skull size would lead to more difficult births, and that the parallel legs of upright posture, with the birth canal positioned between them, limit the possibilities for an accommodating enlargement of the pelvic opening. Thus, the argument continues, selection favors the earlier birth of a less fully developed—a *fetalized*—infant, and a consequent and correlatable condition of *neoteny,*[13] a slowing of rates of development, and retention of juvenile features. Neoteny has often been identified as the significant point of differentiation between humanity and its closest primate relatives.

What sense can be made of neoteny as the trope of the human condition? It is effectively a comparative organismic retardation, a *slowing* or arresting of mortal time, in which the reversal of childbirth plays the role of an escapement mechanism. Of course, the proximate "causes" of the condition— relatively large head size and small pelvic size—are, as fetal characteristics, also consequences of it. But the circle is wider than that, for each of these "causes" is integrally linked to meaning as perception and its expansion into a macrocosm. Neoteny replicates itself as part of a total phenomenon (fig. 22).

Each component of third-order trope is itself an epoch of figure-ground reversal, and each replicates the effect of the whole phenomenon. The cultural dialectic mediates and arrests the formation of mental images through the means of collective reference points; they become epochal perceptions in conventional value space. Language, the figure-ground reversal of thought, makes it necessary that the reference points, and the

13. Stephen Jay Gould, *Ever Since Darwin: Reflections in Natural History* (New York: W. W. Norton, 1977), chap. 7. In the following chapter Gould presents a discussion of the type of argument cited here.

perception within them, be learned *in the world*—hence early birth, and the development of brain laterality *after* birth. Sexuality, the figure-ground reversal of image and body, "arrests" the adult body physically and behaviorally at the point of reproduction.[14] The neoteny that results from the activating clo-

FIGURE 22: Embodiment, the third power of trope.

sure of the trope in the head-loins reversal is thus the realization of a total systemic effect.

The trope of meaning encompasses the meaning of trope: neither nature and culture, nor God and man, nor any of hundreds of other symbols constitutes the true core of a human culture. Rather, its contained and containing form does; the core of every culture is the single idea, or epoch, of humanity.

14. Testosterone seems to be integrally involved with *both* brain laterality and the development of epigamic traits.

References

Barclay, William. *The Lord's Supper*. London: SCM Press, 1967.

Bardon, Geoff. *Aborginal Art of the Western Desert*. Adelaide: Rigby, 1979.

Bergson, Henri, *Time and Free Will: An Essay on the Immediate Data of Consciousness*. Translated by F. L. Pogson. London: George Allen & Co., 1912.

Egloff, Brian J., and Resonga Kaiku. *An Archaeological and Ethnographic Survey of the Purari River (Wabo) Dam Site and Reservoir*. Port Moresby: Office of Environment and Conservation and Department of Minerals and Energy, Papua New Guinea, 1978.

Evans-Pritchard, E. E. *The Nuer*. Oxford: Oxford University Press, 1940.

Fabian, Johannes. *Time and the Other: How Anthropology Makes Its Object*. New York: Columbia University Press, 1983.

Feeley-Harnik, Gillian. *The Lord's Table: Eucharist and Passover in Early Christianity*. Philadelphia: University of Pennsylvania Press, 1981.

Freud, Sigmund. *The Interpretation of Dreams*. London: The Hogarth Press, 1953.

Gardner, Howard. *The Shattered Mind*. New York: Vintage Press, 1975.

Geertz, Clifford. *The Interpretation of Cultures*. New York: Basic Books, 1973.

Gimpel, Jean. *The Medieval Machine: The Industrial Revolution of the Middle Ages*. New York: Holt, Rinehart and Winston, 1976.

Gould, Stephen Jay. *Ever Since Darwin: Reflections on Natural History*. New York: W. W. Norton, 1977.

Harnack, Adolph. *Outlines of the History of Dogma*. Translated by E. K. Mitchell. Boston: Beacon Press, 1957.

Julesz, Bela. *Foundations of Cyclopean Perception*. Chicago: University of Chicago Press, 1971.

Kripke, Saul A. *Naming and Necessity*. Cambridge, Mass.: Harvard University Press, 1980.

Lovejoy, C. Owen. "The Natural Detective." *Natural History* 93, no. 10 (October 1984):24–28.

Macdonald, A. J. *Berengar and the Reform of Sacramental Doctrine.* London: Longmans, Green, and Co., 1930.

MacLean, Paul D. "A Triune Concept of the Brain and Behavior." In *The Hinks Memorial Lectures,* edited by T. Boag and D. Campbell. Toronto: University of Toronto Press, 1973.

Mauss, Marcel, *The Gift.* Translated by Ian Cunnison. Glencoe, Ill.: The Free Press, 1954.

Mumford, Lewis. *Technics and Civilization.* New York: Harcourt Brace, 1959.

Munn, Nancy. *Walbiri Iconography: Graphic Representation and Cultural Symbolism in a Central Australian Society.* Ithaca: Cornell University Press, 1973.

Ong, Walter, J. *Ramus: Method and the Decay of Dialogue.* Cambridge, Mass.: Harvard University Press, 1958.

Ricoeur, Paul. *Time and Narrative.* Translated by K. McLaughlin and D. Pellbauer. Chicago: University of Chicago Press, 1984.

Sahlins, Marshall. *Stone Age Economics.* Chicago: Aldine Press, 1972.

Schneider, David M. "Notes toward a Theory of Culture." In K. Basso and H. Selby, editors, *Meaning in Anthropology.* Albuquerque: University of New Mexico Press, 1976.

———. *American Kinship: A Cultural Account.* Chicago, 1980: University of Chicago Press.

———. *A Critique of the Study of Kinship.* Ann Arbor: University of Michigan Press, 1984.

Sennett, Richard. *The Fall of Public Man.* New York: Alfred A. Knopf, 1977.

Spencer, Baldwin, and F. J. Gillen. *The Native Tribes of Central Australia.* New York: Dover Publications, 1968.

Sperber, Dan. *Rethinking Symbolism.* Translated by A. L. Morton. Cambridge: Cambridge University Press, 1975.

Summers, David. *The Judgment of Sense: Studies in the Language of Renaissance Art.* Cambridge: Cambridge University Press, 1986.

Turner, Victor W. "Body, Brain, and Culture." *Zygon* 18, no. 3 (September 1983):221-45.

Vaihinger, Hans. *The Philosophy of As If: A System of the Theoretical, Practical, and Religious Fictions of Mankind.* Translated by G. K. Ogden. London: Routledge and Kegan Paul, 1968.

Wagner, Roy. *The Curse of Souw: Principles of Daribi Clan Definition and Alliance.* Chicago: University of Chicago Press, 1967.

———. "Mathematical Prediction of Polygyny Rates among the

Daribi of Karimui Patrol Post, Territory of Papua and New Guinea." *Oceania* 42, no. 3 (March 1972):205–22.

———. *Habu: The Innovation of Meaning in Daribi Religion.* Chicago: University of Chicago Press, 1972.

———. "Analogic Kinship: A Daribi Example." *American Ethnologist* 4, no. 4 (1977):623–42.

———. *Lethal Speech: Daribi Myth as Symbolic Obviation.* Ithaca: Cornell University Press, 1978.

———. *The Invention of Culture.* Chicago: University of Chicago Press, 1981.

Zuckerkandl, Victor. *Sound and Symbol: Music and the External World.* Translated by W. R. Trask. Bollingen Series XLIV. Princeton: Princeton University Press, 1969.

Index